Capacity Building Framework

Capacity Building Framework

A values-based programming guide

Brenda Lipson and Martina Hunt

INTRAC
International NGO Training and Research Centre

INTRAC, the International NGO Training and Research Centre, was set up in 1991 to provide specially designed training, consultancy and research services to organisations involved in international development and relief. We aim to improve NGO performance by strengthening management and organisational effectiveness and by exploring policy issues.

First published in 2008 in the UK by:

INTRAC
Oxbridge Court, Osney Mead
Oxford
OX2 0ES
United Kingdom

Tel: +44 (0)1865 201851
Fax: +44 (0)1865 201852
Email: info@intrac.org
Website: www.intrac.org

Copyright © INTRAC 2008: reprinted 2009

Designed and typeset by Grounded Design
Tel: 01993 880028
www.grounded-design.co.uk

Cover designed and produced by Jerry Burman
Tel: 01803 845562

Printed in Great Britain by CPI Antony Rowe, Chippenham, Wiltshire

Acknowledgements

It is important to recognise the enormous contributions made by members of civil society organisations, support organisations and donor agencies who have participated in INTRAC's capacity building activities over the years. The challenges they have presented us and the experiences they have shared have enabled the authors to develop much of the material contained in this practical guide. We would also like to acknowledge our colleagues, past and present, within INTRAC – all of whom have contributed in different ways to this publication. In particular, the capacity building specialists and associates who have engaged in the consultancy work, training courses and programmes which have generated material that we have drawn upon in writing this guide.

Thanks are also due to the members of the reference group that helped steer us in the early days of shaping this guide, and to other capacity building specialists who have acted as sources of inspiration or critical sounding boards as we have pursued this journey. Similarly, thanks to our loved ones who have been invaluable sources of support. Finally, we gratefully acknowledge the financial support for this publication which was provided primarily through the Dutch Government's grant to INTRAC's Praxis Programme.

Brenda Lipson and Martina Hunt, June 2008

Contents

Introduction 1

Part One   **Clarifying the concepts** 6

Chapter 1   **What is capacity?**
               Dimensions of capacity 9

Chapter 2   **Organisational capacity**
               Understanding organisations 14
               Capacity indicators 19

Chapter 3   **Variations in dimensions of capacity**
               Organisational types 24

Chapter 4   **Capacity building**
               'Capacity development' and 'Capacity building' 31
               Capacity building definitions 33
               Capacity building policies 34
               Capacity building and change 36
               Power and capacity building 37

Part Two   **Working with values** 39

Chapter 1   **Organisational values and principles**
               How organisational values shape capacity building programming and
                  implementation 41

Chapter 2   **Relationships**
               Establishing relationships 47
               Power within relationships 48
               Power and partnerships in capacity building 50
               Negotiating relationships in capacity building 51
               Maintaining relationships 52

Chapter 3   **Values and principles expressed in organisational policies**
               Existing organisational policies 54
               HIV/AIDS policy and capacity building programming 55
               Gender and capacity building programming 58

Chapter 4   **Statement of principles for capacity building programming**
               Why a statement of principles? 61
               Starting the process 62
               The principles 64

Chapter 5   **Learning and change**
               Factors which enable learning 67
               Factors which inhibit learning 72
               Implications for capacity building programme design 72

Chapter 6   **The value and principles of capacity builders**
               What is a change agent? 74
               Values and principles of the change agent 77

Chapter 7   **Agendas**
               Identifying agendas 83
               Answering 'Capacity building for what?' 86

Part Three	**Designing and implementing a capacity building programme**		89
Chapter 1	A programmatic approach to capacity building		
	What do we mean by the 'programmatic approach'?		92
	Different programmatic approaches		94
	Benefits of the programmatic approach to capacity building		97
Chapter 2	Mapping and analysis		
	The purpose of mapping or scoping exercises		99
	Methods and tools for mapping		101
	Analysis		107
Chapter 3	Scope and objectives		
	Levels of intervention		109
	Goal and objectives		122
	Scope of intervention		114
	Which CSOs will participate?		115
Chapter 4	Intervention strategies and activities		
	Choosing strategies		117
	Capacity building activities		118
	Choosing appropriate activities according to the capacity building intervention level		119
	Factors affecting choice of strategies and activities		128
Chapter 5	Three common programming approaches		
	Civil society sector/sub-sector strengthening programmes		131
	Partner capacity building programmes		134
	Organisational Development (OD)		136
	Key similarities and differences across the three approaches		140
Chapter 6	Support provision and roles		
	An overview of supply and demand		143
	The supply of capacity building services		145
	The 'best practice' role		148
	Choosing the optimal roles		149
Chapter 7	Resourcing a capacity building programme		
	Funds and funding sources		151
	Specialised in-house expertise		152
	Broad knowledge base		153
	Staff competencies		154
	Relevant relationships		155
Chapter 8	Monitoring and evaluation		
	Learning		157
	Indicators		158
	Monitoring and evaluation		161

Final thoughts 171
General reading 173
Appendix – Capacity building programme – Framework guide 175

Introduction

This guide aims to provide a comprehensive framework to aid the design and implementation of capacity building programmes. It combines conceptual exploration with practical step by step suggestions, challenging the reader to consider the wider issues behind the practical process of designing and implementing a programme.

The lack of a framework for capacity building programme design and implementation may at times allow a multiplicity of meanings and interpretations to emerge. Furthermore, the question, 'what is capacity building?' remains subject to 'continued conceptual muddiness'. However, more recently there have been efforts to reach a consensus on good practice. These efforts to gain clarity have contributed to a more secure foundation on which to base this book.

The guide aims to:

- share a comprehensive framework for designing and implementing capacity building programmes
- provide practical reference material for INGO and CSO staff and for local support providers working with them on capacity building programming
- influence programme staff and decision makers regarding good practice in capacity building and in particular raise awareness of how values and power issues influence the design and implementation of capacity building programmes
- share examples of different approaches operating in diverse contexts by the use of relevant case studies and examples.

The guide is a companion to the 2007 INTRAC publication *Capacity Building for NGOs: Making it Work*, by Rick James and John Hailey, which provides an overview on the current debates on civil society capacity building. It analyses both the concepts and experiences of organisational capacity building and makes strategic recommendations for future directions.

Critical questions

Throughout the guide there are references to two key questions:

'Capacity building for what?' and **'Capacity for what?'**

The importance of these questions and how to answer them are key factors that influence the design of capacity building programmes.

The first question provokes the reader to think about the underlying purpose of engaging in capacity building work. It is a question which is aimed at eliciting a reflection about the deeper motivations and values that are at play – the 'why' of capacity building. These may be the motivations of organisations engaged in this work and also of individual actors. Without awareness of the agendas of the organisations and individuals involved, there is little **conscious** capacity building taking place – and without consciousness, little possibility for openness to reflection and change.

The second question helps to focus the mind on the precise nature of the specific capacity building initiative. The reader is pushed to consider what are the **specific** capacity areas that the initiative is trying to address. It is a programming question, rather than a values one like the first question. It is aimed at helping define the 'how' of capacity building.

The reader is encouraged to constantly ask how clear they are about the answers to these two questions.

Who the guide is for?

This guide aims to meet the needs of a range of readers, including:

- INGOs who are developing capacity building programmes aimed at their partners or as part of broader civil society development work.
- International civil society organisations such as global membership movements, federations etc who are developing capacity building programmes aimed at their individual member organisations.
- Support providers working with the INGO/ICSO capacity building programmes.

In addition, official agencies (both dedicated civil society units and sector or geographic units), other donors (such as foundations and trusts) and local NGOs/CSOs may find it a useful reference book.

Structure of the guide

The guide is divided into three parts:

Part One sets in place some core references regarding the 'what' question, i.e. what are capacity and capacity building? It also focuses on organisational capacity, and looks at models for understanding different types of organisations and how they develop.

Part Two focuses on the values and principles that shape the programme and emphasises the importance of understanding and making explicit some of the hidden values that affect the programme. It explores issues of values and power at the individual, relational and organisational levels. There are overviews on learning, and on working with explicit statements of principles applied to capacity building work. Part Two concludes with an outline of how values and principles provide the reasons why organisations become engaged in capacity building –the answer to the 'capacity building for what?' question.

INTRODUCTION

Part Three explores the design of the programme, the 'how' of capacity building. It takes the reader through a process of designing and implementing a programme, beginning by looking at the concept of working programmatically and then going through the different stages of the design process. Part Three considers issues of context and environment; the goal and objectives of the programme (in particular in relation to the answer to the 'capacity for what?' question); the potential scope and levels of intervention, types of strategies and activities, resource issues and learning and accountability.

Capacity building framework

A framework can be understood as:

- an underlying structure which supports a variety of elements
- an expression, in a simplified and accessible manner, of a complex process. This is often achieved by grouping similar elements into categories
- a set of assumptions, concepts, values, and practices that constitutes a way of viewing reality.

We use a notion of 'framework' for capacity building programming that covers all three aspects. The aim is provide an overview on the process of **understanding** the motivations behind the initiative, **analysing** the influences upon it and **thinking through** the programming choices to be made.

The benefits of using a framework are that it:

- provides a systematic way of thinking through options
- facilitates a coherent approach
- enables choices to be made that are appropriate to the purpose and context of the initiative
- helps communication with stakeholders.

We find it most useful to use the notion of a framework as a human body**:**

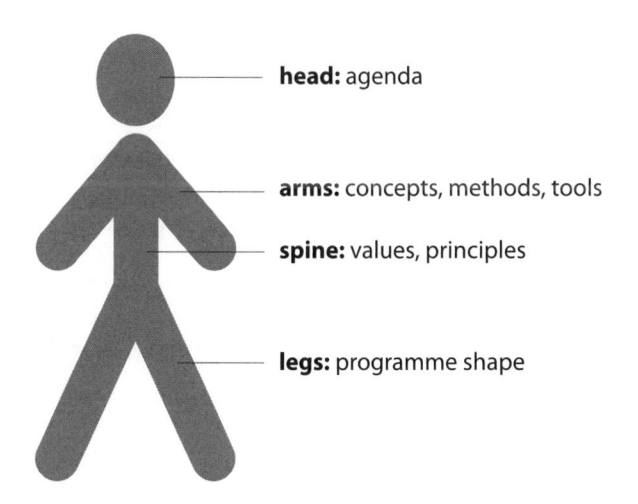

head: agenda

arms: concepts, methods, tools

spine: values, principles

legs: programme shape

The **head** is the **agenda** behind the initiative to engage in capacity building work. It is the answer to the 'capacity building for what?' question which needs to be addressed before embarking upon a programme. The head is the reasoning behind why any organisation or individual becomes involved. It would tend to be phrased in 'big picture' language such as capacity building for; 'poverty reduction'; 'democratisation'; 'disaster risk reduction'; 'HIV/AIDS prevention'.

> **Critical thoughts**
>
> How clear and explicit is your agenda? What are the influences shaping it?
>
> How broad or focused is your answer to the 'capacity building for what?' question? Who is involved in answering this question?

The **arms** are the **concepts, methods and tools** that you will be using. They range from the broad understanding of organisational capacity and capacity building, through various methodological approaches and tools that can be applied according to specific needs and contexts.

Examples include:

concepts: (on) what is capacity; what is an organisation; what is civil society and a civil society organisation; (on) the role that context plays in regard to organisations; what is capacity development and capacity building; what is organisation development and institutional development etc.

definitions: what your organisation decides is its working reference of the concepts.

methods: for all phases of the programme including mapping/assessment; diagnosis; design; intervention strategies; approach to implementation (e.g. facilitative, directive); monitoring, evaluation and impact assessment.

tools: specific instruments, exercises, processes etc used which are appropriate to the method and objectives identified.

> **Critical thoughts**
>
> Do you have access to a range of conceptual literature? How engaged are you in conceptual debates – do you need to be?
>
> Does your organisation have agreed definitions or a broad understanding about the concepts?
>
> Do you have a good collection of applied reference materials illustrating methods and tools?
>
> Have you thought about how strong your arms are?

The **legs** refer to the **programme shape** and ground the framework. They involve making choices about :

- Programme nature – is it stand-alone, cross-cutting, 'notional' etc
- Scope and target population
- Levels of intervention
- Goal and objectives
- Timeframe
- Strategies and activities and choice of appropriate methods and tools
- Monitoring, evaluation and impact assessment
- Roles and relationships
- Resourcing

> **? Critical thoughts**
>
> How far does the programme shape of this capacity building initiative fit with your organisation's overall approach to programming?
>
> How are you working to make sure the shape is appropriate to specific contexts?

Finally, the **spine** is what holds the whole body together. Here we locate the **values and principles** that guide everything – the agenda and the choices about concepts, working definitions, programme design and implementation. The values and principles may be located at the level of the organisation itself, and also at the level of the individuals involved in the design and implementation of the work. The spinal column will reflect the core values, vision/mission, culture etc of the organisation. It will also be influenced by the context within which the organisation is operating.

Examples of values and principles include:

- Working with an explicit commitment to structural change in society
- A high value placed on processes which are empowering
- A high value placed on results, reflected in the organisational culture
- Principles of equality
- Human rights principles as a reference point for programming

> **? Critical thoughts**
>
> Are you aware of how your organisation's values and culture may influence your capacity building work?
>
> Are you aware of the influence of your own values and principles?

Despite all humans having similar skeletal structures, the actual body form may vary enormously between individuals. Much of the body form is influenced by the **context** in which it has developed – whether it be the specific chromosomes that shape our individual make up or the environmental factors that encourage certain strengths to develop. Likewise, with capacity building programming it will be the context in which this takes place, and in which the eventual work will be implemented, that will play a huge role in determining the final body form.

The chapters in this book are linked to different parts of this framework, which the reader can identify by the following icons.

Head   Arms   Spine   Legs

How to use the guide

The guide sets out easy referencing to a wide range of topics and materials:

- With the body icon clearly indicated, so the reader is aware of how the guide takes them through each part of the framework.

- Critical thought boxes are used to prompt the reader to review their own and their organisation's practice. These questions can be used as a learning process by individuals; they can be shared in programme teams, with partners and with managers. They challenge the reader to think about some of the fundamentally important questions that often go unanswered or left implicit.

- Signposting is used to help the reader navigate through the book, and to highlight other parts of the book where, for example, a point is discussed in more detail or from a different angle.

- Case studies and examples are used to reinforce learning from practice.

- End-of-chapter summaries are a useful reminder of what has been covered.

- Recommended reading is provided for each chapter. They may present alternative views or approaches to the subject, and thus help the reader identify those that are in tune with their own values and overall approach.

Part One
Clarifying the concepts

Introduction

Part One relates to the 'arms' of the framework, and explores the concept of capacity to enable the reader to clarify their understanding of the term. Being clear on the concept will ensure clear and coherent approaches to capacity building programming. Chapter 1 looks at **what is capacity** and offers a definitional framework which guides the thinking of this book; Chapter 2 introduces some models for understanding **organisational capacity** as a fundamental basis for strong arms and strong capacity building programming; Chapter 3 highlights that while there are common characteristics to organisations, there are various **organisational types** where capacity may be expressed differently; and finally Chapter 4 focuses on **what is capacity building**?

In its simplest form, capacity is an 'ability to' or 'power to' do or be. **Chapter 1** sets out some common themes and definitions; shares INTRAC's understanding, which guides the conceptual framework for this book; and helps the reader to determine their own understanding of capacity.

For a capacity building programme to be both sustainable and contribute to strengthening civil society, it is necessary to have a good understanding of the nature of organisational capacity. **Chapter 2** explores the key elements that define an organisation and how it develops, with particular emphasis on the context in which the organisation is operating. It illustrates the range of capacities that an organisation needs at the various stages in its development, and introduces a number of models which can be referred to when designing and implementing capacity building programmes.

Organisations are complex, organic and ever-changing. Social change organisations not only try to influence the environment in which they work but are also influenced by that environment. Organisations can not function effectively in isolation, they need to invest in their relationships with other organisations within their environment, such as civil society organisations, funders, governments, and the private sector.

Further capacity analysis is needed depending on the type of organisation. **Chapter 3** breaks down the term 'civil society organisations' into various types and identifies variations in the expression of capacity for the more common organisational types that capacity building programmes may be working with – including networks and faith-based or community based organisations.

Applying a standardised description of organisational capacity to all organisations is inappropriate. Diversity, even within one organisational type, means that it is necessary to develop appropriate capacity indicators according to the form and function of the organisation. Consideration should also be given to how capacity indicators may differ according to different contexts, for example post-conflict; high vulnerability to natural disaster; highly centralised systems of governance.

Chapter 4 looks at how capacity develops and the conscious process involved in capacity building, as well as introducing the related issues of development, change and power. The chapter highlights the following:

Capacity development is the increased ability and power to do something in particular (functional capacity), or increased resilience and autonomy (intrinsic capacity). It is a broad term which conveys the notion of a change process with no involvement of 'agency' i.e. where no purposeful capacity strengthening intervention has taken place.

Capacity building indicates purposeful and conscious efforts to bring about capacity development. Capacity building refers to a process that has a clear purpose and set of specific objectives. It is a **structured process** that is framed around the answer to the question **'capacity for what?'**

Organisations are developing 'definitional frameworks' as an alternative to attempting to encapsulate their understanding of the terms 'capacity building' or 'capacity development' in one phrase. Part One helps the reader to have greater clarity about their own definitional framework before undertaking capacity building programming.

Chapter 1
What is capacity?

'We believe that capacity is found at different levels – with individuals, groups, organisation-wide and the broader systemic level. The specific expressions of capacity can be diverse – it can be a resource capacity; a relational one; a behavioural one; a skill; an infrastructural capacity etc. Capacity is not located in a vacuum – it has an applied nature, often explored through the "capacity for what?" question. We believe that capacity is fluid and that it can decrease as well as increase.'
(INTRAC)

Concepts, methods and tools

In its simplest form, capacity is understood as an 'ability to' or 'power to' do or be. This chapter sets out some common themes and definitions, and shares INTRAC's understanding of capacity, to help the reader determine their own understanding of capacity. The chapter relates to the 'arms' of the body. Being clear on the concept (i.e. having 'strong arms') will allow the reader to ensure clear and coherent approaches to their capacity building work.

Dimensions of capacity

Ability and power

The 'ability to'

Capacity has historically been viewed as a human resource term, such as an individual's capacity to do, to achieve, or to develop, and is most often referred to in terms of competencies and capabilities. More recently, capacity refers to capability at different levels, i.e. an organisation, system or society, to function or to perform. Some common definitions within the development sector include:

> 'The ability of individuals and organisations or organisational units to perform functions effectively, efficiently and sustainably.'
> (UNDP)

> 'The ability to perform tasks and produce outputs, to define and solve problems, and make informed choices.'
> (European Commission)

These definitions reflect **instrumental or functional approaches**, with a heavy emphasis on performance related notions of capacity. They are closely associated with a model focused on the effective absorption of external resources made available to southern CSOs by others operating within the formal aid system.

> 'Capacity is the ability of [an] organisation to implement and manage projects, to exercise financial and product accountability as per Northern specifications, to employ and train staff competent to undertake specific tasks, and to report on their work in ways which are acceptable to their donors … The ability to deliver specified products, often according to others' specifications.'
> (Allan Kaplan, CDRA)

Part Two, Chapter 2

The 'power to'

The focus on 'ability to' do (something) misses the dimension of power. Thus, although someone may have the *'ability to'* do something, they may not have the opportunity to put this into practice because someone or something (institutions, governments, legislation, and context) may be constraining them. Thus one may not have the *'power to'* as in the following example:

> Individual x has the ability (skills and infrastructure) to create networks with other organisations via the internet, which will improve the capacity of her organisation to communicate and build relationships. However, the context (the political environment) in which the organisation is operating does not allow this. Access to internet is blocked and thus, despite having the ability to communicate the organisation does not have the power to do so. Hence the organisation does not have full capacity to communicate and build relationships.

So the capacity of an organisation to achieve its goals depends both on the individual or the organisation's ability and their power.

> **Critical thoughts**
>
> Does your organisation have the ability but not the power to achieve your goals – how is this manifested?
>
> Is this the case for organisations you work with on capacity issues – what are the implications for your work with them?

'Doing' and 'being' – Capacity is 'intrinsic' as well as functional

The most common usages of the term 'capacity' associate it with action, i.e. the 'ability' or 'power' to *do* something. However, describing capacity only as performance-related is insufficient – it is also concerned with the ability or power 'within', i.e. to *be* or to exist – its **'intrinsic' or 'robust' capacity.** This is linked to an entity's inner need for survival. For example, an organisation may have the capacity to perform effectively and efficiently, but it requires additional capacities to survive.

'Capacity ... [is] the ability of an organisation to function as a resilient, strategic and autonomous entity ... [which is] capable of sovereign focus and direction, of strategising and innovation, of responding with flexibility and adaptability to changing circumstances, and of acting decisively to impact on, and change, their circumstances and social context.'
(Allan Kaplan, CDRA)

This definition enables us to identify capacities related to resourcefulness, resilience, confidence, adaptiveness, creativeness and survival. These capacities are intangible and more subtle. Strategies designed to develop such capacities are less obvious, and require more than one-off interventions.

Capacity is expressed in different forms

Capacity may be expressed in different forms, such as:

Human capabilities, for example attributes that can be found in individuals, their skills, knowledge, experience, values, attitudes and world view.

Relational capabilities, for example shared value or belief systems, networks of groups with a common cause, sharing information.

Resource capabilities, for example, tangible resources such as money, buildings and computers or intangible resources, such as time and opportunity.

Capacity is located at different levels

As well as different forms, capacity can be located at a range of inter-linked levels. These levels, known as 'scales of human action' are located from the individual through many forms of collective organised endeavours to sectors and social institutions. The importance of considering this dimension when working with capacity issues is illustrated in this example:

> **Case example**
>
> Organisation X recently carried out a self-assessment which identified capacity gaps in relation to its planned five year programme of work. One key gap concerned networking at different levels and in various forms. The context was one of societal change and of a civil society sector emerging from state control. Few CSOs had previously been able to network and now when they could, there was limited experience in building up networks. There was also an attitudinal issue, as those engaged in civil society work were suspicious of collaborating with others. Within individual organisations these attitudes affected the sharing of information, trust and openness amongst colleagues. At the individual level, in addition to the reluctance to invest in new relationships, people did not necessarily have the skills and experience to do so.

As well as locating capacity at individual, organisational and sectoral levels, as this example shows, capacity is also located at the societal level, i.e. the context in which an organisation operates. Any society has a range of elements which facilitate the actions of organised citizens and civil society, for example, favourable legislation, tax exemptions, or consultation policies that encourage dialogue. This is the 'enabling environment', discussed further in Part Three.

> Part Three, Chapter 4

Capacity is applied

Whether capacity is the ability or power to do something, or whether it is the ability or power to be or to exist – there is a purpose to capacity. It does not operate in a vacuum but is applied within a context. This dimension focuses on the key question: **'capacity for what?'**

Using the metaphor of child development, each action has a purpose – learning to walk, to have the capacity to be mobile; learning to talk, to have the capacity to communicate. Similarly, an organisation may need a new capacity in response to its changing environment, for example, the ability for staff to use email in order to communicate more effectively on a global scale.

> **Critical thought**
>
> Have you asked the 'capacity for what?' question before designing your capacity building work?

Capacity is fluid (ebbs and flows)

Capacity evolves over time and can both develop or decline. Certain factors contribute to capacity increasing, such as a conducive working environment, where people are valued and time and money is invested towards increasing capacity by, for example, skills training or learning seminars. Equally, certain factors may contribute to reduced capacity. For example, organisations lose skills when staff leave the organisation for better conditions elsewhere as sometimes happens when local CSOs lose staff to INGOs. We will explore this dimension of capacity in more detail in chapter 4 when looking at 'capacity development'.

> **Critical thought**
>
> Have you explicitly considered the ways in which your future interventions may contribute to decreasing capacity?

SUMMARY

This chapter has helped the reader understand the concept of capacity and thus create 'strong arms' for the body framework. The key concepts are :

- Capacity can be understood in different ways, often referred to as instrumental or functional capacity and intrinsic or robust capacity.
- Capacity varies in form and can relate to human, relational and resource capabilities.
- Capacity can be found at different levels, from the individual, group, organisation and societal levels.
- There is always a purpose to capacity, hence the underlying question 'capacity for what?'
- Capacity is fluid and can decrease as well as increase.

> **Critical thoughts**
>
> Are you clear about your understanding of capacity and is your understanding shared with colleagues and your organisation?
>
> How do the dimensions of capacity impact on the design and implementation of your capacity building programme?

RECOMMENDED READING

Further views on capacity can be found in Morgan, P. 'The Concept of Capacity', 2006, a draft paper produced as part of a research programme into capacity and located at www.ecdpm.org

Chapter 2
Organisational capacity

Concepts, methods and tools

Understanding organisational capacity is pivotal to successful capacity building programming. Before exploring organisational capacity issues it is important to understand organisations and their development. This chapter presents various models to assist the reader in designing and implementing their capacity building work. It looks at the key elements that define an organisation, and how it develops and survives, with particular emphasis on the context in which the organisation is operating. It also illustrates the various capacities that an organisation needs at different stages in its development.

> 'Without taking heed of the need for the sustainability of activities and the importance of capacity building and organisation strengthening to achieve this, almost any development support is likely to have short-lived results.'
> (Sida)

Understanding organisations

Organisations are complex, organic and ever-changing organisms, that function within differing contexts which interact with the organisation both positively and negatively. Social change organisations are 'open systems' which not only try to influence the environment in which they work but are also influenced by that environment. Organisations can not function effectively in isolation, they need to invest in their relationships with others, such as CSOs; government; donors; and private sector, regional and international bodies.

When considering organisational capacity it is helpful to think of a variety of elements (specific capacities) which enable the system to fulfil its purpose and function as a resilient, strategic and non-dependent entity. These elements can be located within three different organisational dimensions and are contextually influenced. When we look at an organisation's overall capacity to be successful in its mission, we try to understand this capacity in relation to:

- the demands and pressures from the external environment
- its programme performance
- its internal functioning and
- its relationships.

ORGANISATIONAL CAPACITY

This is expressed in the 'Three Circles' model:

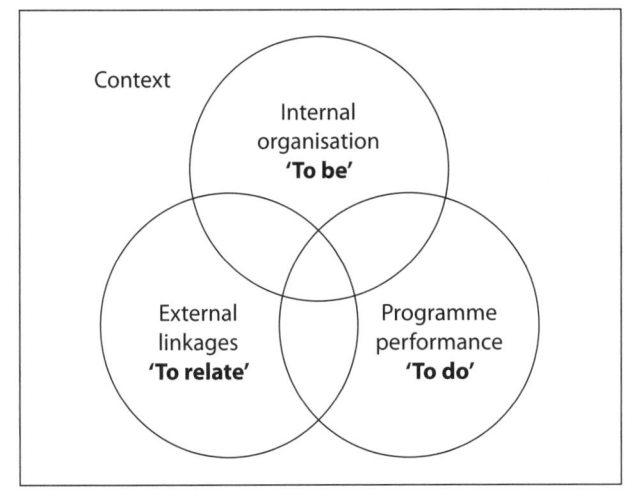

```
Context
         Internal
         organisation
         'To be'

External            Programme
linkages            performance
'To relate'         'To do'
```

Source: INTRAC, 1993

The overarching principle in the model is the interlocking nature of all three areas of organisational capacity. So, for example, if an organisation's capacity to relate to other organisations is poor, or its leadership is weak, this will affect its performance. Likewise there is a continuous interaction between the organisation and surrounding context – each impacting on the other.

The CSO's **programme** (or **'to do'** circle) is the work that it does – for example, human rights, health, poverty alleviation, education. This dimension includes a series of capacities related to project management; technical skills and knowledge/expertise in the topics which form the content of the organisation's programme; competencies in research, policy influencing etc.

However, for an organisation to effectively deliver the programme and fulfil its mission it needs to have a strong vision of what it is striving for, based on core values; effective leadership; a comprehensive strategy; appropriate internal systems; competent staff etc. These are some of the specific capacities of the second organisational dimension – its **internal** functions or **'to be'** circle. The capacities in this dimension are related to the overall organisational performance and sustainability.

Part One, Chapter 1

In addition, an effective CSO needs to have **positive (helpful) external relationships** with other organisations and institutions – it needs to be able **to relate**. CSOs cannot achieve change by working in isolation. The organisation needs to manage its relationships strategically, and staff need to be competent in relevant skills such as negotiation and communication. There is a direct correlation between the quality of a CSO's external relationships and its impact on development.

The critical element in this model is the **context** or **environment** within which the CSO is operating. Understanding how the organisation interacts with the external context is viewed as increasingly important in analysing and managing CSO capacity. An organisation's ability to understand its environment, interact easily with it, and anticipate and manage subsequent change – is a key capacity which enables such organisations to adapt and survive more readily.

The internal organisation

The metaphor of an onion can be used to look more specifically at the internal organisational capacities that a CSO needs.

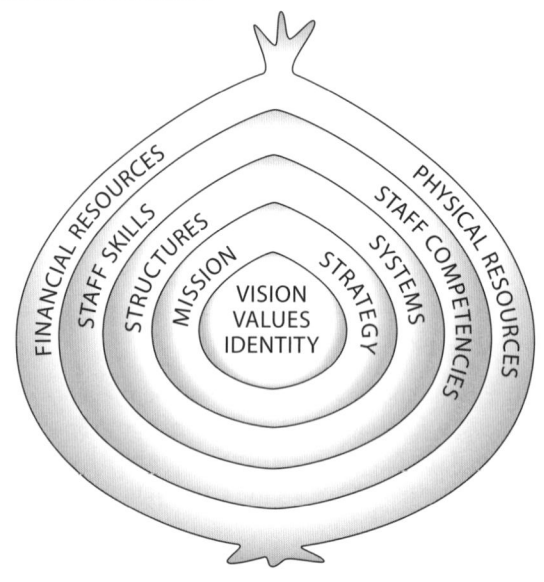

Source: James, R. *Demystifying Organisational Development*, INTRAC, 1998

An onion grows in layers of skin from the centre (core) outwards. In organisational terms this means that growth in the organisation should be coherent with the heart (core) of the organisation. This is its identity, culture and world view, based on the founding values and vision. These provide the basis and legitimacy of the organisation's actions. The next layer of organisational skin is the organisation's purpose (mission) and strategy – what the organisation hopes to do about achieving the changes in the world that they think are important. These must be directly and explicitly related to the changes conceptualised in their vision:

> 'The first requirement for an organisation with capacity, the "prerequisite" on which all other capacity is built, is the development of a conceptual framework which reflects the organisation's understanding of the world. This is a coherent frame of reference, a set of concepts which allows the organisation to make sense of the world around it, to locate itself within that world, and to make decisions in relation to it.'
> (CDRA)

Outside that, there are the **structures** and **systems** (such as monitoring and evaluation systems, human resource systems, financial management systems) that help to operationalise the strategy and make an organisation work. The next layer is capacity contained in the **human competencies** required to take the strategy forward, i.e. carry out the activities and manage the organisation. These capacities are most visible as individual staff competencies, skills and abilities. The outer layer (what the rest of the world sees most easily) are the **physical** and **financial resources**, for example, money, buildings, vehicles and equipment.

This model shows clearly how healthy organisations grow on the basis of a strong core. It also indicates that if you change these layers, the changes should be coherent with the core, but also may require change in the other layers. An example of this is that if you develop a strategy to work in new thematic areas it will be important to develop or recruit staff with the new competencies required. Effective **organisation change and growth** must be based on **coherence** and **consistency** between these layers.

This model also illustrates that not only is capacity less visible towards the core, but that interventions here **penetrate deeper into the organisation and are often more complex and difficult**. Indeed, CSOs themselves often struggle to analyse their needs beyond immediate resource deficiencies, and yet their most serious and long-term problems are much more deep-rooted and not easily solved just through an injection of funds. The onion metaphor allows us to understand how an organisation may rot from within (for example, loss of founding vision), and yet the outer layers may still appear to be in place. It may be easier to solve the problem of a lack of physical resources than that of self-serving values or an unclear purpose, but capacity building interventions may not have the desired impact unless issues closer to the core are addressed.

> **? Critical thought**
>
> One final aspect of the onion metaphor is that when you cut an onion, it makes you cry … working on capacity issues at the heart of an organisation can sometimes be a sensitive and painful process.

The lifecycle of an organisation

Just as living organisms have a lifecycle, so too do organisations. One model that helps identify the different phases of organisational growth and some characteristics and capacity issues that coincide with each phase is shown below:

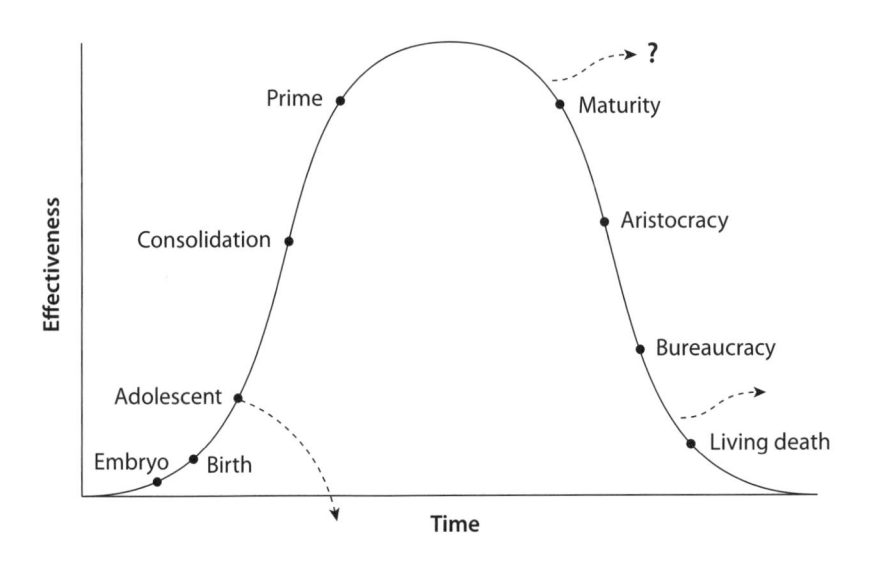

The two axes suggest that over time performance increases but will eventually begin to decline. This reflects the human lifecycle.

Embryo

Many organisations start with a dream, an idea – for example, one person or a group decides they want to provide a service for the community. This is not yet an organisation and will require a lot of nurturing to make it to the next stage.

Birth and infancy

The organisation is born: only very basic policies or systems are in place. There is no track record and in the early days the people involved with it do everything themselves – running the activities, raising funds, writing reports. They are often opportunity-driven and vulnerable to changes in the external environment. Decisions are commonly taken collectively and many, if not all, of the staff are volunteers.

As the organisation becomes known, more opportunities present themselves. This may lead to an organisation doing too many and too diverse a range of initiatives. They need to learn to prioritise. There is still a strong collective responsibility and everyone knows what each other is doing.

Adolescent

As the organisation expands and becomes more successful, it inevitably experiences 'growing pains'. New staff have to be recruited and new systems developed. The founders often try to control every aspect of the organisation, but such control becomes less and less feasible. There is a need to depersonalise the leadership and develop standardised administrative systems. Some founders are unwilling to let go and the resulting crisis can tear the organisation apart, or some founders decide to leave.

Consolidation

If the organisation comes through this crisis, it often devotes its resources to establishing a sound management and administrative base. Personnel policies and financial management systems are established and priority is given to long-term planning and coordination.

Prime

This leads on to a stage when the organisation finds itself in its most effective period: a strong strategic approach with clear goals, well-established support systems and committed staff. There are risks that the organisation might become inward looking and question whether their priorities are right.

Maturity

The effectiveness is still there but the commitment to the vision might start to weaken. The culture may be less innovatory and become **risk averse**. Ideally, the organisation needs to renew itself, re-engage with its vision, learn from the people they are working with, and move back into the 'prime' stage. If it does not …

Aristocracy

The decline begins. The efficiency will still be there and the organisation will probably keep its good reputation over time. But the organisation will gradually lose contact with reality. The enthusiasm and creativity will disappear. Serious problems will occur but these will be ignored or hidden. These underlying problems will have to be dealt with. Any revival will have to be dramatic and is often associated with a change in senior management.

Bureaucracy

Sooner or later the aristocratic organisation will be hit by bad news: major sources of funding may refuse further support, the media may launch an attack, users may band together to protest. People start to fight and search for scapegoats. The better people, since they are feared, are fired or leave while others hang on long after they cease to perform a useful function. If the organisation can continue to get funding, it moves into the bureaucratic phase where there is no vision, the programmes are secondary and the emphasis is on forms, procedures and paperwork. Any revival has to be traumatic and radical surgery is needed; otherwise …

Living death

The organisation will lose the confidence of its constituency and donors and will die. Although some bureaucracies never get there, they just go on and on …

Organisational regeneration

For organisations this cycle can manifest itself in the rise and fall of performance. However, unlike the natural lifecycle in humans, organisations can rejuvenate or reinvent themselves in new forms (mergers or breakaways) or change leadership and bring new life to the organisation. The model above illustrates that organisations need to start a new lifecycle while they are still on the upward curve.

Energy is required to start a regeneration process and although this may be hard to mobilise when the organisation appears to be doing well, it will be more difficult to mobilise if the organisation goes into decline. Organisations need to prepare for the future by ensuring strategic thinking is taking place, and by constantly exploring questions and considering alternatives. If not, they may get stuck at certain phases of development and without having a clear strategy for change may not move on to achieving more.

The different stages of organisational maturity help us understand where an organisation is and also set realistic goals about achievable changes. It may not be realistic to expect that a simple capacity building intervention will enable huge leaps forward but is more likely to help an organisation move to the next level of development.

Capacity indicators

Within each of the three organisational dimensions (internal, programme and relational) there are a number of different capacities. It is useful to define indicators which describe in more detail what each capacity looks like. Whilst there may be some generic indicators, it is useful for such indicators to be defined specifically for each organisation according to:

- Development stage of the organisation
- Organisational type (e.g. an intermediary NGO, a grassroots community organisation or a network)
- External context
- Culture

> **Critical thought**
>
> The definitions of the indicators of an organisation's capacity can be highly subjective and may be influenced by power dynamics and value judgements. Thus care is needed to understand who is defining these and how.

One example of how indicators may be influenced by power dynamics are capacity indicators which describe an effective local NGO working in children's health programmes. If these are defined by the donor agency alone, they may emphasise characteristics which are of greatest interest to that agency e.g. high level of project management skills, regular reporting, capacity to monitor quantitative data. Perhaps if defined by the local NGOs, the descriptions would emphasise other characteristics such as the use of empowering methodologies during the project cycle, participative approaches to reporting or capacity to capture stories of impact.

Indicators may be expressed at different levels of complexity and detail. Below are some examples of capacity indicators that were developed by Omani NGOs during a capacity building workshop. These are at a basic level of detail and complexity, and were developed to be used in tracking progress during a management development programme.

Examples of capacity indicators

To be:

- A clear statement of our vision and mission, which is used to guide our decision making.
- Clarity about our target groups and how to reach them.
- An internal structure in place which is appropriate for our work.
- Clear and differentiated roles and responsibilities for our Board, staff and volunteers. These are written and shared.
- All the resources necessary to succeed in our mission.
- We respect and observe the values, customs and traditions in society whilst doing our work.
- A wise leadership, who know our objectives and seek to achieve them.
- We benefit and learn from our previous experiences in order to develop our potential and effectiveness.

ORGANISATIONAL CAPACITY

To do:

- A strategy or medium-term plans in place for our work projects.
- A clear operational plan related to that strategy, which we implement.
- Plans and projects are continuously monitored, and revised when necessary.
- The capacity to change and adapt as a result of lessons learnt, or changing circumstances.
- We evaluate the success of our strategic plan at the end of its period.
- Use methods which encourage the participation of the beneficiaries in all phases of our project work.

To relate:

- We have identified all the different individuals, groups, communities, organisations who are affected by, or have a strong interest, in what we do.
- Good relations with donors supporting our plans.
- Community leaders trust our organisation and believe in our cause.
- Regular communications with similar regional and international NGOs.
- Strong relations with other Omani NGOs with whom we regularly share experiences.
- A positive relationship with government authorities.

Capacity indicators for different phases of an organisation's growth

The evolutionary process of an organisation's development must be captured in the definitions of the capacity indicators. The recognition of different and unequal levels of capacity is essential for effective capacity building work.

The grid below illustrates capacity indicators at different stages of development. It is part of an organisational assessment tool developed by INTRAC and partners during work on a civil society strengthening programme in Cyprus. This grid illustrates three capacity areas in the 'to relate' dimension.

Capacity	Strategic analysis of appropriate relationships (identification and selection according to organisation's mission and objectives)	Building positive two-way relationships	Negotiations (with government, donors, community leaders etc)
Level 1 – Embryonic	No systematic analysis of stakeholders and their interests. Little recognition of the need to carefully identify with whom to have relationships, their purpose and nature, and their contribution to organisation's objectives. Relationships initiated in an ad hoc manner.	Most relationships weak or not performing well.	Little or no negotiating capacity (skills, experience, confidence, resources)

Level 2 – Developing	Informal analysis of key stakeholders. Organisation recognises the need to carefully identify appropriate relationships. However this is rarely reflected in the initiation of relationships in practice.	Most relationships functioning at a basic level of joint activities. Little regular communication, sharing of information or analysis of shared interests.	Minimal capacity to negotiate. A few one-off positive results identified. Little connection made to organisational objectives.
Level 3 – Moderately developed	Organisation undertakes formal analysis of stakeholders. It applies its understanding of relationships to identify and initiate potential relationships, but not consistently. A number of different types of relationships are identified.	Responsibility for managing each relationship not clearly assigned. Most relationships functioning at a basic level but some are well-managed and performing well. Need for a strategic approach to communication with others starts to be recognised.	Good skills being developed and confidence growing. More systematic analysis of results of negotiating efforts. Identified need for strategic approach.
Level 4 – Well-developed	Formal analysis of stakeholders and their interests is incorporated in discussions. Organisation uses a consistent and systematic approach to identify and initiate potential relationships. Different types of relationships are actively pursued. Some review and prioritisation of existing relationships.	Responsibility for managing each relationship clearly assigned. Many relationships healthy and performing well. Strategic communication and information sharing becomes integrated. Some successes with building deeper-level commitment to organisation's mission.	Organisation developed a range of skills and experience in successful negotiation, and reviews and builds on these experiences. Developing a strategic approach to negotiating, linked to organisational mission and objectives.
Level 5 – Exemplary	Formal analysis of stakeholders and their interests incorporated in decision making. Organisation uses a consistent and systematic approach to identify and initiate potential relationships. It regularly reviews and renegotiates existing relationships (including planned exit strategies where appropriate). Established relationships are prioritised.	All relationships well managed, and everyone is satisfied their objectives are being met. There is regular, open communication; committed interaction and collaboration. Parties within the relationships regularly review their nature and progress.	Organisation is fully confident in its negotiating capacity, and is seen as a model by other CSOs. It has a working strategy for negotiating, and can clearly identify the ways in which its successful negotiations has contributed to organisational objectives and mission.

When assessing the capacity of an organisation to effectively relate with others, it is necessary to break this down into specific individual capacity areas. The grid shows three of these – capacity to analyse and select relationships in a strategic manner; capacity to build positive two-way relationships, and capacity to negotiate within relationships. The assessment of the organisation's relational capacity will need a judgement about the level of development of each one of these specific capacities. It is very unlikely that an organisation will have equal levels of development across each of the capacity areas.

SUMMARY

A good understanding of the nature of organisational capacity is essential for a capacity building programme to be both sustainable and to contribute to strengthening civil society, This includes consideration that:

- organisations are continuously growing, adapting and evolving, having and requiring different capacities at any one time. Identifying appropriate capacity indicators for each growth phase will guide the organisation's development.
- the most resilient organisations have a strong inner core as well as a balance of key capacities in the different organisational dimensions – (programmes, internal functioning and relationships) – and the ability to live comfortably in its own environment.
- organisations are more likely to survive and be healthy if they are able to renew and regenerate by anticipating changes needed and to think strategically about the future.

RECOMMENDED READING

Most of the reading material referred to in the General Reading section has specific chapters or sections on organisational capacity. In addition, these are some shorter articles:

Kaplan, A, 'Shifting the Paradigms of Practice', 1997, article on CDRA website, available at www.cdra.org.za

Kaplan, A, 'The Development of Capacity', 1999, a development dossier available at www.un-ngls.org

Chapter 3
Variations in dimensions of capacity

Concepts, methods and tools

The previous chapter introduced some models for understanding organisations and introduced the notion of working with a range of capacity indicators, according to the phase in an organisation's evolution. Whilst the three circles framework can be applied to **all** organisations, further capacity analysis is necessary depending on the **type of organisation**. This chapter breaks down civil society organisations into various organisational types and identifies variations in expression of capacity for some of the more common organisational types.

Organisational types

Civil society capacity building programmes may be working with different types of organisations that have differences in their form and function, or different emphasis of purpose. These types include:

- Intermediary NGOs
- Umbrella bodies or apex organisations made up of member organisations, often around a certain type (e.g. NGOs, faith-based organisations (FBOs) and professional bodies)
- Sector, thematic or issue-based networks or coalitions
- Grassroots or community-based organisations (CBOs)
- Self-help groups
- Identity based organisations (e.g. indigenous peoples' organisations)
- Cooperatives or other similar member-based organisations
- 'Informal' traditional associations, such as temple groups, burial societies etc.

Capacity indicators for different organisational types

Applying a standardised description of organisational capacity to all organisations may be inappropriate. The following illustrates some examples of different key capacity indicators for:

1. Networks

Networks can be broadly defined as 'loosely organised groups of CSOs that share values and ideologies' (James, 2004). Networks have many different forms, depending on their purpose, for example, advocacy coalitions, funding consortiums and learning networks. CSO networks have a number of strategic roles open to them and demanded of them by different stakeholders. For example, they coordinate members; advocate with government and donors; build capacity of members; and broker funding for members.

This diversity, even within one organisational type, shows how necessary it is to develop the most appropriate capacity indicators according to the form and function of the network.

> **? Critical thoughts**
>
> Experience tells us that …
>
> Capacity indicators will not work as a checklist to be applied across the board to all networks.
>
> The exact expression or definition of each indicator will vary from network to network, as will the relative importance of each capacity.

The following grid, adapted from Wilson-Grau and Munez, gives an example of capacity indicators for international social change networks.

	Organisational dimensions		
	To be	To do	To relate
Examples of capacity indicators	The diversity of members is appropriate for the network's purpose and strategies	The objectives of the network have been agreed by all members and are underpinned by shared values and beliefs of the network	The network emphasises building relationships of trust internally and externally
	The structure is light, facilitative and supportive – rules are minimal	The activities of the network reflect the range of political positions in the network	The network actively seeks to strengthen communication channels between members and outside the membership
	Organisational culture is in tune with network principles – the network thinks and acts as a network not as an institution	The operational outputs of the network are more than the sum of the activities of the individual members	The network invests time and money in developing internet linkages and direct contact with a range of similar networks internationally

This emphasises the need to work with specific capacity indicators in accordance with the nature of the network. However, it is possible to make some general comments about those capacity areas which particularly express the differences between networks and individual organisations. It is likely that capacity indicators for networks will emphasise the following in addition to the more generic organisational capacities:

- clear decision making procedures which indicate how differences of opinion amongst individual members are resolved

- clarity about membership issues, e.g. criteria for inclusion; representation on the governing body; executive body's accountability to membership
- common standards expected from member organisations
- clarity on the scope and parameters for the network's actions in comparison with activities undertaken by individual member organisations
- clarity on all aspects of internal communications: frequency, scope, form etc
- clear delineation of the roles and responsibilities of the secretariat, in relation to the work of the member organisations.

2. Faith-based organisations

The main distinction between a FBO and other CSOs is its relationship with a religious institution or faith group. As with networks, FBOs vary in form and function. For example, some FBOs are attached to one particular church whilst others have links with many religious bodies. The first column below illustrates different ways in which FBOs relate with the main religious institution. Here, capacity indicators will vary along a continuum, some examples of which are given in the other three columns.

		Organisational elements		
		Identity values and beliefs	**Governance**	**Resources**
Examples of capacity indicators for:	**FBO within religious institution**	There is absolute coherence in the values, beliefs and identity of the FBO and the religious institution.	Religious leaders effectively combine their spiritual responsibilities with those related to the management and activities of the FBO.	The religious institution is firmly committed to ensuring full funding for the FBO activities.
	FBO partially within religious institution	There is coherence in the values and beliefs of the FBO and religious institution, and clarity about the different identities of the two entities.	Religious leaders effectively delegate day to day authority for FBO and are clear on the distinctions between their spiritual remit and leadership role and that related to the governance of the FBO.	FBO receives partial core funding from the religious institution. It is able to complete its financial targets by raising funds from a variety of other sources.
	FBO separate from religious institution	FBO has a clearly independent identity. FBO stakeholders are clear about which values and beliefs are shared with the religious institution.	Religious leaders are clear on the autonomous nature of the FBO governance structure. They are happy to participate as a member of the Board if invited.	FBO funding is entirely independent of the religious institution. Any applications for funding to the institution only take place when funding criteria allows.

Another characteristic of many FBOs is their use of faith-based references in their organisational policies, strategies and operational instruments. It is likely to be important to consider these references when developing capacity indicators.

> **Examples of specific capacity indicators with faith references:**
>
> **To be:**
>
> - All organisation-wide policies express clearly the theological basis on which the subject is founded (e.g. non-discrimination policies based on certain theological references which indicate the value placed on treating all people in an equal manner).
>
> **To do:**
>
> - Programme strategies contain references to relevant spiritual teachings, which clarify and guide organisational decision making.
>
> **To relate:**
>
> - The organisation's partnership policy clearly expresses the fundamental faith-based origins for its approach to partnerships.

The specific expressions of organisational capacity appropriate to FBOs are different from those of secular entities. Similarly, the wider faith institution to which they belong will influence the definition of the capacity indicators. Consideration of these differences is needed for the development of a capacity building programme that includes working with FBOs.

> **? Critical thoughts**
>
> Have you considered how the capacity indicators will reflect the faith base of FBOs that may be participating in the capacity building programme?
>
> Who will be involved in the identification or development of these indicators? The FBO alone or will others from the wider faith institution be involved?

3. Community-based organisations

CBOs may take diverse forms. In this book we understand CBOs to be grassroots organisations created and managed by local members primarily for their own interests and benefit, and operating with a strong, shared identity as an independent entity. Such organisations may be fluid – disappearing and re-emerging in different ways. Often they are not formally constituted, i.e. do not have legal registration under existing civil society regulatory frameworks.

It is important to be aware of the danger of automatically transferring to CBOs those capacity indicators that have been defined for other individual CSOs operating at a different level, such as intermediary NGOs.

> **Examples of capacity indicators:**
>
> **1. An indicator to express a strong delivery capacity in the programme or 'to do' area:**
>
> This may be expressed, for intermediary NGOs, in terms of knowledge of, and effective use of, project cycle management methods. For a CBO, it may be more relevant to refer to the organisation having a strong capacity to effectively identify the changes it wishes to secure and plan its activities accordingly.
>
> **2. An indicator to express strong strategic capacity:**
>
> It may not be appropriate to refer to a CBO's capacity to engage with formal strategic planning processes – a common indicator which is used for intermediary NGOs or networks. It may be more appropriate to define the capacity in terms of strategic thinking.
>
> **3. An indicator to express human resource capacity:**
>
> Most indicators developed with NGOs in mind will refer to paid staff, and to formal procedures which must meet legal norms operating in the country. CBO indicators for human resource capacity will need to place greater emphasis on the capacity to recruit and retain unpaid, voluntary resources – whether in the form of volunteers or members of the organisation.

As with networks, there are some areas which are of particular importance to grass-roots organisations and which will require specific attention when defining their indicators for strong capacity. These include:

- the degree of 'rootedness' in the community: within the 'to be' dimension of a CBO, the capacity to build and maintain a strong constituency.
- the capacity to hold leaders accountable to the membership in ways that are appropriate to the cultural context.
- the capacity to identify and build appropriate relationships is critical for individual CBOs, who without this may operate in an isolated and weakened fashion.
- a strong cultural and organisational identity is critical for a CBO to have legitimacy within its own cultural context. This identity provides the basis for autonomy and to resist inappropriate external influences, tutelage etc.
- the capacity to identify power differentials within the organisation, and to work to address imbalances wherever possible.

> **? Critical thought**
>
> Have you identified the **crucial** differences in capacities between the various types of organisations you will be working with?

Influences of context

As indicated in the three circles framework, understanding an organisation as an 'open system' emphasises the importance of how an organisation interacts with its context and in turn how the context influences and shapes the organisation. Consideration should be given to how capacity indicators may differ according to variations in contexts, for example:

- Conflict and post-conflict
- High vulnerability to natural disaster
- Low-trust environments
- Highly centralised and controlled systems of governance

⟷ Part One, Chapter 1

In addition, four key environmental characteristics have been identified that shape the definition of capacity indicators. They indicate how an organisation might require certain types of capacities according to their context. These are:

1. **Stability** – an organisation's context can range from *stable* to *dynamic*. What is important is the degree of predictability in the context which will influence the way in which an organisation plans. An example of a specific capacity indicator relevant for organisations operating in unstable environments could be:

    The organisation can respond and adapt quickly to unpredictable events, having in place flexible systems and appropriate response mechanisms that are brought into action when required.

2. **Complexity** – ranging from *simple* to *complex*. A complex environment is one where the organisation needs to make use of knowledge and other inputs from a diverse range of sources, to provide a complex range of services.

3. **Service diversity** – from *integrated* to *diversified*. This refers to an organisation's ability to respond to either an identified community or a broad range of social settings. An example of a specific capacity indicator relevant for organisations working in a context which is characterised by highly diversified services could be:

    The organisation maintains a high quality of services to its clientele and is known in the community for being able to respond positively to the specific needs of elderly, disabled and minority groups.

4. **Hostility** – from *supportive* to *hostile*. When considering this element, it is important not to assume that differences of value and purpose, or disparities in resources and influence, necessarily indicate environmental hostility. The environment only really becomes extremely hostile when the operations and the purposes of one particular organisation and that organisation only, are actively threatened.

Source: Adapted from Mintzberg, H (1983)

> **Critical thoughts**
>
> Have you considered the specific issues related to the context in which you are working?
>
> What are the implications for the definition of capacity indicators appropriate to organisations working in that context?

SUMMARY

This chapter breaks down civil society organisations into various organisational types and identifies variations in expression of capacity for the more common types that capacity building programmes may be working with. Key points are:

- Applying a standardised description of organisational capacity to all organisations is inappropriate. Appropriate capacity indicators need to be developed according to the form and function of the organisation.
- Consideration should be given to how capacity indicators may differ according to variations in contexts.
- Four key environmental characteristics shape the definition of capacity indicators – stability, complexity, service diversity and hostility.

RECOMMENDED READING

Ashman, D. *Supporting Civil Society Networks in Institutional Development Programmes*, AED Center for Civil Society and Governance, 2005

Hofstede, G. *Cultures and Organisations: Software of the Mind*, McGraw Hill, 1991

Mintzberg, H, *Structure in Fives: Designing Effective Organizations*, PH Enterprises, 1983

Tashereau, S and Bolger, J. *Networks and Capacity*, ECDPM, 2006

Chapter 4
Capacity building

Previous chapters have explored the concepts of capacity and organisational capacity. This chapter looks at how capacity develops and the conscious process involved in capacity building, as well as introducing related issues of development, change, performance and power. As in previous chapters, this chapter focuses on strengthening the 'arms' of the body framework. Having a strong understanding of the concept of capacity building and its relationship to change is critical to effective capacity building work.

Concepts, methods and tools

'Capacity development' and 'Capacity building'

Readers may be familiar with either of these terms, and will probably have been exposed to some of the debates about the limitations or advantages of using each one in turn. INTRAC uses both terms, but places a different meaning on each:

> 'The development of organisational capacity can be consciously catalysed (capacity building) or may emerge and be expressed as patterns of changed practice or behaviour (capacity development).'
> (INTRAC)

INTRAC refers to **capacity development** as the increased ability and power to do something in particular (functional capacity), or increased resilience and autonomy (intrinsic capacity). It relates to Kolb's experiential learning cycle below:

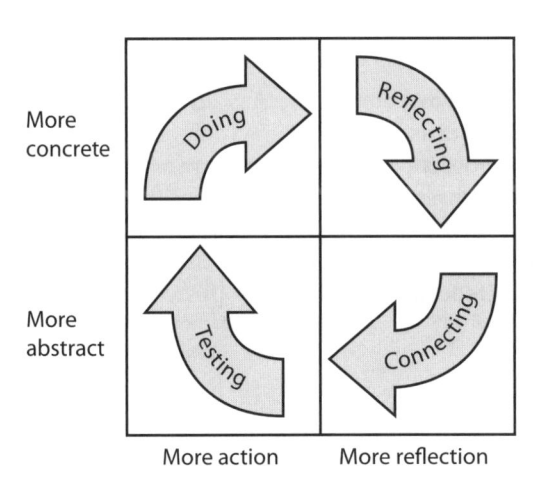

More concrete / More abstract

Doing — Reflecting — Connecting — Testing

More action / More reflection

The learning cycle illustrates that capacity develops as new, constructive elements that are located in and/or emerge from practice. Reflection and review are essential to embedding these new elements and to identifying developments that have emerged in practice.

◆ Part Two, Chapter 5 and Part Three, Chapter 7

> ### 👁 Case example: developing capacity
>
> Organisation Y is a local intermediary NGO whose mission is to increase well-being of women in marginalised communities, by supporting the development of their livelihoods opportunities. Before the tsunami, they worked exclusively in Madras. However, when the tsunami hit nearby coastal communities, the organisation responded. After a year of working with women in the affected communities, the organisation reviewed their activities.
>
> Before the tsunami, the members had not felt that they had the appropriate knowledge and expertise to work in rural areas. They believed that the situation of the urban poor and marginalised women required specific knowledge and skills sets that could not be applied to very different contexts. However, the review findings showed how the members of the organisation had adapted their knowledge and skills base, and had been able to identify activities that were relevant and appropriate to the needs of women based in small coastal communities.
>
> This review highlighted developments in the organisation's capacity to be adaptive, flexible and open to innovation. It also showed that technical skills and knowledge-based capacities had grown as a result of the very human desire to respond to others' distress. The organisation therefore decided to continue to work with coastal communities as a permanent programme area.

INTRAC uses the term **capacity building** to indicate purposeful and conscious efforts to catalyse capacity development. There is no assumption that 'building' means starting something from scratch. 'Capacity building' suggests a purpose to the activities, whereas 'capacity development' may be viewed as a broader term which can cover a process with no involvement of 'agency' i.e. no purposeful intervention.

Thus, capacity building refers to a process that has a clear purpose and set of specific objectives. It is a **structured process** that is framed around the answer to the question 'capacity for what?'. The process is designed following an initial diagnosis or capacity assessment. This diagnosis phase can be part of the capacity building process, depending on the methodology used. Due to the complex and, at times, ambiguous nature of capacity building processes, it may not always be appropriate to think that a planned, linear design will ensure predetermined outcomes. This will be explored further in Part Three, Chapter 3.

Capacity building definitions

There are a range of definitions for capacity building, including:

> 'To improve the ability of NGOs in developing countries to be able to deliver more effective development impacts in their communities.'
> (International Working Group on Capacity Building, World Bank)

> 'Capacity building is an ongoing process – a conscious intervention to help people, organisations and societies improve and adapt to changes around them. Performance and improvements are taken in the light of mission, objectives, context, resources and sustainability.'
> (Rick James, 2000)

> 'The process by which individuals, organisations, institutions and societies develop abilities (individually and collectively) to perform functions, solve problems, and set and achieve objectives.'
> (UNDP)

> '… the provision of training and consultancies for the primary target group (the poor) (i.e. self help groups and their associations), but also for the secondary target group (state and non-governmental intermediary organisations).'
> (GTZ)

> 'An ongoing process by which people and systems, operating within dynamic contexts, learn to develop & implement strategies in pursuit of their objectives for increased performance in a sustainable way.'
> (CIDA)

> 'A process whereby people and organisations improve their performance in relation to their mission, context, resources and sustainability.'
> (Aga Khan Foundation)

The definitions highlight some common characteristics of capacity building:

- It is a conscious intervention – specifically designed in response to an assessment, diagnosis or analysis. It has specific change objectives, and will establish the means to measure the degree to which those objectives have been achieved.
- It builds on existing capacity. Capacity building work should not be assuming that it is 'starting from scratch'.
- It is ongoing – very often long-term, with no clear cut-off points.
- It is focused on many levels – from the individual through individual organisations, networks, coalitions, civil society sector and societal level.
- It is context specific –,capacity building work must be relevant and appropriate to the external environment within which it is taking place.
- It needs to be sustainable, and seek to establish sustainable results.

Increasingly, organisations are developing 'definitional frameworks'. These are a collection of statements which build the picture of how that organisation understands the concepts of capacity and capacity building. This is one way of overcoming the constraints of a single, definitive statement which attempts to encapsulate the complexity of these concepts.

Part Two, Chapters 4 and 7

> **Critical thoughts**
>
> How clear is your organisation's understanding of capacity development and capacity building?
>
> It is for you to decide what makes sense for your organisation. Importantly, it needs to be agreed and shared.

Capacity building policies

Working with a definitional framework can be expanded further, as some organisations may find it more helpful to work with a broad capacity building policy which may include some, or all, of these elements:

- the organisation's understanding of the concept and definitions of capacity building
- a description of how capacity building is located within the organisation's development philosophy and practice (the agenda)
- the preferred methodological approaches
- the roles that the organisation's staff play in relation to capacity building initiatives
- any agreed priorities on the scope of the organisation's capacity building work (in terms of sectors, organisations, partners, geographic or thematic focus)
- lessons learnt from past experience
- guiding principles based on the organisation's values as well as drawing on sector-wide 'good practice' principles
- any resourcing-related policy
- description of how other organisation-wide policies will be implemented within the capacity building work.

CAPACITY BUILDING

> ### 👁 Case example
>
> 'The CHF Capacity Building Approach articulates and describes CHF's philosophy and approach to capacity building. It is based on 45 years of development experience and lessons learned from designing and implementing hundreds of projects with developing country partners throughout the world. These guidelines have been developed to:
>
> - guide CHF program managers and technical staff in designing, implementing and monitoring capacity building programming in their projects
> - describe CHF's capacity building approach and methodology to current and prospective partners
> - explain the rationale for our capacity building activities and approaches to donors and other development stakeholders.'
>
> Source: The CHF Capacity Building Approach, 2007

The body framework used in this guide could serve as the basis for developing an organisational capacity building policy. The 'head', 'arms' and 'spinal column' would form the core of the policy. The 'legs' would tend to be the application of the policy in a specific programme.

In a recent survey of the current approaches being taken by INGOs in their capacity building work, the overwhelming majority of respondents did not have a policy framework for their work. Even where capacity building specialists were employed, few were engaged to develop a formal capacity building policy. Nevertheless evidence suggests there can be several benefits from developing such a policy framework. These include:

- consistency and coherence in the capacity building work undertaken by different departments of the organisation
- enhanced learning opportunities by articulating and disseminating capacity building lessons through a common language
- conceptual, definitional and methodological reference points
- increased learning at sectoral level as policy frameworks enable a shared understanding of capacity building work
- a comprehensive reference point for any future capacity building interventions
- legitimacy for the capacity building programme and approach, confidence for the capacity building support provider that they are supported at organisational policy level.

> ### ❓ Critical thoughts
>
> Have you experienced difficulties in capacity building initiatives due to insufficient guidelines on capacity building work?
>
> Is there agreement about capacity building principles and approaches within your organisation or network of organisations? If not, how does this impact on your work?

Capacity building and change

Capacity development and capacity building both involve change. This may happen at any level:

- Changes occur within individuals as they learn new skills or develop new perspectives based on increased knowledge/information.
- Within individual organisations, seeking to increase capacity in any, or all, of the three dimensions will necessarily mean bringing about changes in existing ways of working.
- Likewise groups of organisations will have to realise that how they relate to each other may have to change if they are to be more effective in achieving their shared goal.
- At the sector level, building the capacity to respond to new openings and space for engagement with other sectors may include changing mindsets or beliefs.

Part One, Chapter 2

> **Critical thoughts**
>
> Engaging with capacity building means engaging with change. How far are you analysing this process of change?
>
> Are you considering changes in all dimensions of the organisations you are engaging with and the context within which they are working?

Analysing the process of change is an important step in understanding capacity building. Changes may be understood as:

- results of triggers of events
- emerging from new patterns of practice

Triggers for change

These can be a range of both externally and internally generated factors that act as catalysts for a reaction. The nature of the response may vary – it may be strategic, reactive, tactical and so on.

Examples of external triggers are:

- political change or crisis of governance in the country
- natural disasters
- changes in donor policies.

> Examples of internal triggers are:
> - financial crisis
> - changes in key leadership positions
> - changes in terms and conditions for staff.

It is critical to understand the unique mix of variables that may make up the triggers for any specific change and to draw out the implications for the system as a whole.

Change emerging from new practice

Change can also emerge from practice without necessarily involving a trigger. This understanding focuses more on the notion that the system itself might generate change. New patterns may be detected in the ways in which different organisational space is occupied (e.g. space for learning; for discussion and decision making). New patterns of behaviour between individuals or within groups may also be seen. The mix that makes up that organisational system may itself constantly generate new and dynamic patterns that are expressions of organisational change.

These change processes may be consciously managed or happen subconsciously as **continuous processes of adaptation**. In this way, capacity development can be seen as an organic process and also as a result of 'agency', that is, the conscious action involved in capacity building.

Part Three, Chapter 4

Power and capacity building

> 'Capacity building is a conscious approach to change which has radical and far-reaching implications not only for skills and behaviours, but also power dynamics within and between organisations'
> (James, 2001).

Power dynamics are present when people try to make sense of the changes around them; when choices are made about what and how to change; and when the conscious efforts to change challenge the status quo. Power dynamics operate at all levels from the individual, to the team, organisational, network, sector and societal level.

Part Two, Chapter 2

Fundamentally, change involves a process of negotiation involving individuals within the system. This process is one in which individuals describe their personal interpretations of what is happening and together construct a shared reference point for the new situation. It is a process in which power dynamics are intrinsic; individually held value and belief systems may clash and the core organisational values and identity may be tested. It can take place within one individual organisation, or within networks or cross-sector work. Capacity building processes demand highly adaptive behaviour on the part of those leading them.

Part Two will explore power issues in more depth. However the importance of these issues to capacity building needs to be recognised early on in the process, particularly in relation to change.

SUMMARY

This chapter looks at how capacity develops and the conscious process involved in capacity building, as well as introducing intrinsically related issues of development, change and power. Key points include:

- **Capacity development** is the increased ability and power to do something in particular (functional capacity), or increased resilience and autonomy (intrinsic capacity). It is a broad term which can also cover a process with no purposeful intervention.
- **Capacity building** indicates purposeful and conscious efforts to catalyse capacity development. Capacity building is a structured process that has a clear purpose and set of specific objectives. It is framed around the answer to the question 'capacity for what?'
- Organisations are developing definitional frameworks as an alternative to trying to capture in one phrase their understanding of 'capacity building' or 'capacity development'.
- Analysing the process of change is an important step in understanding capacity building. Changes may be understood as results of triggers of events, and emerging from new patterns of practice.
- Capacity building is a conscious approach to change which has very radical and far-reaching implications for both skills and behaviours, and power dynamics within and between organisations.

RECOMMENDED READING

Black, L (2003), 'Critical Review of Capacity Building Literature and Discourse' in *Development in Practice,* Vol.13, No.1, Feb pp116-119

Fukuda-Parr, S, Lopez, C and Malik, K (eds). *Capacity for Development – New Solutions to Old Problems,* UNDP, Earthscan, 2002

James, R. *Power and Partnership: Experiences of NGO Capacity-Building*, INTRAC, 2001

Postma, W (1998), 'Capacity Building: The Making of a Curry', in *Development in Practice*, Vol. 8, No. 1

Some useful tools related to managing change can be found at:

www.change-management-toolbook.com

'Capacity for Change' – paper based on outcomes of a workshop held in September 2007. Available at www.ids.ac.uk

Part Two
Working with values

Introduction

Part Two focuses on the **backbone** of the capacity building framework – the values and principles which shape the programme. Imagine a body without a spinal column – it is what joins all the other parts together to make it function as a whole. **Values and principles** shape and guide the design and implementation of capacity building work, implicitly and explicitly, both at the individual and organisational level. Part Two aims to enable the reader to work with both explicit and more hidden values and principles so that programming decisions are both relevant and appropriate to the individual, programme and organisation as a whole.

At the level of individuals engaged in capacity building initiatives, **self awareness** is fundamental to understanding the ways in which values and principles may influence behaviour, attitudes and the choices made. At the organisational level, the **identity** of the organisation which is funding, sponsoring or implementing the work will also impact on the programming decisions. Thus its core values and beliefs, which are at the heart of its culture, vision, mission and guiding policies, will play a critical influencing role.

Values are the priorities and preferences of individuals and groups that reflect what is important to them. They are the 'motivators', the 'engine rooms' for our actions and will direct and change our perception, affect our decision making and trigger our emotions. Values can also be expressed as **principles**, or standards of behaviour.

This guide understands 'values' to be:

> Ideas and qualities that are informed by, and in turn inform, beliefs, principles and aspirations that are important to the actors involved in capacity building initiatives.

Often one word or term is used to indicate a value, for example, inclusiveness, equality, justice, poverty elimination etc. But that word could be understood to mean very different things by different people. A comparison of value statements of NGOs and private sector companies would show similar words appearing, but the question arises as to their meaning for the organisations involved.

For example, 'justice' may be important to a capacity building practitioner but the word on its own may not have much meaning for others. The practitioner may put words to what they mean by their belief in the importance of justice. But to also understand how justice is important to this practitioner it would be necessary to see how they actually express it in their beliefs, principles, and aspirations as they go about their work. It would also be necessary to understand the relative nature of justice – what is a fundamental human right to one person is a right that is seen as a privilege to another.

Whilst the international development sector incorporates a large amount of value laden language within general use when discussing visions, missions and strategies, there is far less reference to how values *inform* the process, decision making and actions of the work. Certain assumptions may have been made about a shared culture of specific values and beliefs. Part Two aims to encourage the reader to make explicit the evolutionary process by which certain values and principles influence their capacity building work.

The chapters in Part Two cover the following themes:

- the relationship between organisational values and capacity building (**Chapter 1**)
- how organisational values and principles affect relationships within capacity building initiatives (**Chapter 2**)
- organisational values expressed through specific policies and how these impact on capacity building approaches (**Chapter 3**)
- the process of making values and principles explicit through 'statements of principles' (**Chapter 4**)
- values and principles implicit in learning within capacity building (**Chapter 5**)
- the role of the individual change agent and the self awareness of the practitioner's own values and power (**Chapter 6**). This chapter will be especially of interest to readers engaged directly in providing capacity building services.
- how values and principles influence the reasons why an organisation develops capacity building work in the first place (**Chapter 7**).

Chapter 1
Organisational values and principles

Most of the chapters in Part Two focus primarily on values which are held by the *organisation*, although it is recognised that there is interplay between both individual and organisational values. The models of organisations introduced in Part One emphasised the importance of organisational values, beliefs and world view as being at the heart of an organisation's identity. An organisation involved in capacity building programming will bring with it a set of values and principles which will influence the design and implementation of the programme. Some of these values will be explicit; others will be hidden and may even be unconscious in the organisational psyche. This chapter provides an overview on the impact of some key organisational values on capacity building programming work – the following chapters explore specific elements of this in more detail.

Values and principles

↔ Part One, Chapter 2, three circles and onion models

How organisational values shape capacity building programming and implementation

Organisational values and principles shape capacity building work throughout all the phases of design and implementation. Chapter 7 shows how they come into play with regard to shaping the agendas or reasons why an organisation becomes engaged with capacity building work. The capacity building approaches, definition of goal and objectives, selection of strategies and activities and so on, are all influenced by core organisational values and principles.

↔ Part Three, Chapters 2, 4 and 5

It is important to identify the nature of these values and principles. They may be illustrated by the following set of beliefs about the importance and nature of:

- How change happens in society (at global through to community levels) and within organisations.

> **Case examples**
>
> 1. Organisation X believes that positive changes in society will only happen if there is a strong external 'push' to complement any demands for change from internal actors within that society. This forms part of its core values and is expressed through a vision statement which emphasises international solidarity as a major factor for global peace. This high value placed on the external driver for change will influence choices about the kinds of capacity building strategies to be used (e.g. emphasising international exchanges/networking capacities); the roles to be played by staff members (e.g. playing a strong 'hands-on' delivery role as a direct expression of international solidarity) etc.
>
> 2. Organisation Y places great value on individuals and their contributions to helping organisations achieve their missions. It believes that only if individuals are open and responsive to change, will the organisation itself change and develop. The vision statement refers to a world where civil society organisations are composed of members who are self-reflective, critical and innovative. This strong emphasis on individual level capacities means the approaches taken to the organisational capacity building work will draw heavily on strategies focused at individual change processes (e.g. mentoring, leadership development etc) and success will be measured in terms of individual change as well as organisational performance.

- How the organisation views its own role in those change processes.

> **Case example**
>
> Organisation A is a faith-based organisation which draws on theological references to emphasise its role as 'witness' to poverty and injustice. Because of these strong values of 'accompaniment' to the poor and marginalised in their own efforts to achieve social change, the organisation encourages its staff to engage in long-term capacity building support work with its partners. The work is prioritised towards strengthening the partners' capacity to advocate for change. The approach to the work integrates a strong two-way learning dimension, particularly recognising the importance of the organisation strengthening its own capacities in order to 'witness' more effectively (e.g. focus on capacities to be open to criticism; to reflect and change, and to communicate and advocate effectively).

- Who does the organisation believe should influence the way it operates and in what ways (governments, donors, members, supporters etc)?

> **Case example**
>
> Organisation B is a European membership organisation, and believes that its programme of work should reflect the interests and concerns of its members. As the membership recently expressed its interest in increasing the amount of environmental sector support that the organisation undertakes, the organisation has decided to prioritise its capacity building work towards that sector. Thus, it is engaged in an 'functional' approach to capacity building, identifying its agenda as one which prioritises the strengthening of civil society organisations to combat environmental degradation and climate change.

Other core organisational beliefs which influence how the organisation approaches capacity building include:

- what it believes is a positive relationship in general terms, and 'strong partnerships' specifically
- power dynamics and how the organisation engages with issues of power
- what is understood as 'quality' work
- how the organisation balances results and process, e.g. does the demand for effective, sustainable results outweigh issues of how the results are achieved?

> **Critical thoughts**
>
> Can you identify the range of values and principles at the core of your organisation that may influence the design and implementation of capacity building work?
>
> If not, who do you need to discuss this with?

Values in competition with each other

It is possible for an organisation to hold values that, in certain circumstances, may compete with each other for dominance. It is important to be aware of the risk of competition as it can weaken or undermine efforts to ensure effective capacity building work.

> ### 👁 Case example
>
> Organisation X is a northern INGO which is developing a partner capacity building initiative to be implemented as a 'stand-alone' programme in four regions within its International Programme. The organisation has a partnership policy which lays out the guiding principles for its work with southern CSOs. The organisation also has embarked upon a 'good governance' drive – initiated by the Board – to ensure that the organisation can be confident about the most appropriate and effective use of its resources.
>
> The staff working on the design of the capacity building programme wish to ensure local ownership throughout the process, with the partners taking the lead on decision-making. They believe that the programme must be 'demand led' to achieve the desired changes in organisational health and effectiveness. This commitment is stated publicly and referred to in the planning meetings and design workshops being held in the regions.
>
> However, simultaneously there are internal management directives which ask programme staff to follow new procedures to ensure transparency and effective use of project funds. Staff are now required to obtain more complex financial and narrative reports from partners. It is probable that the new capacity building programme will have to incorporate activities to ensure that the partners comply with the new reporting demands.
>
> Thus, staff on the capacity building initiative have to reconcile two potentially competitive organisational values – 'local ownership' and 'rigorous accountability'. The first value has been expressed in public statements. The second is a more hidden organisational value – the move to good governance being, until now, an internal organisational initiative.
>
> It is vital for the future credibility of the capacity building work that these two values are reconciled. The challenge is not impossible, but its success will depend on:
>
> - staff being clear on how the two values may influence the capacity building in different, and potentially contradictory, ways
> - staff being able to openly articulate that there are these potentially competing demands to their partners
> - there being sufficient trust and commitment to the partnership amongst all the stakeholders, to enable all parties to recognise the need to reconcile the potential contradiction
> - there being sufficient time and opportunity to work together to design an initiative that is fully 'owned' by the partners rather than one that may be felt as responding to the 'imposed' values of the more powerful northern INGO.

Power and control are critical aspects of any development practice. Organisational values, either hidden or explicit, have a bearing on the power dynamics within relationships that the organisation has. Moreover, the hidden values may have significantly more bearing than those that are made explicit by an organisation. The power issue is therefore complex, and measures have to be put in place to counteract the power imbalances that occur within many relationships, otherwise the values that are expressed are not necessarily practiced.

> **? Critical thoughts**
>
> How aware are you of potentially contradictory values that are held within your organisation? Are these values clearly articulated?
>
> In what ways might these contradictions affect the capacity building work?
>
> What steps can be taken to mitigate any negative impact on the work?

Making explicit the core organisational values that impact on the design and implementation of a capacity building programme has benefits at various levels:

- At the organisational level, the staff are aware of the value dimensions that have helped shape the programme.
- At donor/supporter level, negotiations on terms of reference have a clear reference point.
- At partner/client level, the relationship can be established and maintained, with clear expectations of the principles of working together.
- At the individual level (e.g. the capacity building specialist) the organisational values provide confidence in terms of the actions and decisions they make in designing and implementing the programme.

Results versus process values

It is worth highlighting one dimension within the broad range of organisational values – the relative importance and value placed on achieving results in relation to the way that those results are achieved.

This is a tension that significantly influences capacity building practice. The issue may be seen by asking 'what is rewarded in the organisation?'. Is greater value placed on showing individual initiative, winning contracts or obtaining funding or does the organisation value more intangible dimensions of relationship building or the use of empowering methods? Part Three covers the stages in designing and implementing a capacity building programme, each of which is influenced by the organisation's views on the results–process dynamic. In practice, there may be a continuous balancing act between results and process.

For example, it is a well established development principle that empowerment and ownership of the process and outcomes of development come about when the primary stakeholders participate at the heart of the process. The implications are that it takes time and expertise to bring about such a process. In reality the value placed on participation must be balanced with certain operational constraints – perhaps funding and reporting deadlines, staff turnover or organisational procedures.

Being clear on the relative balance between results and process will assist the steps taken to clarify:

- the agenda behind the capacity building strategies and programmes
- the choices made about the means/end of capacity building

- the choices of the ultimate goal and definition of strategies to be employed
- who is involved in design work
- who is seen as the 'driver' of the initiative
- funding mechanisms and reporting deadlines
- the roles undertaken by different actors
- the relationships established
- the levels of internal capacity investment needed to effectively undertake these programmes.

SUMMARY

This chapter provides an overview of the impact of some key organisational values on capacity building programming work. Capacity building approaches, definition of goal and objectives, and selection of strategies and activities are all influenced by core organisational values and principles.

It is important to identify the nature of these values and principles. They may be illustrated by the following set of beliefs about the importance and nature of:

- How change happens in society at large, and within organisations.
- How the organisation views it's own role in those change processes.
- Who the organisation believes should influence the way it operates and in what ways (governments, donors, members, supporters etc).
- What it believes is a positive relationship in general terms, and 'strong partnerships' specifically.
- Power dynamics and how the organisation engages with issues of power.
- The understanding of 'quality' work.
- The balance between results and process.

It is possible for an organisation to hold values that, in certain circumstances, may compete with each other for dominance. It is important to be aware of this potential dynamic as it may weaken efforts to ensure effective capacity building work. Making explicit the core organisational values that impact on the design and implementation of a capacity building programme has benefits at various levels.

RECOMMENDED READING

De Bono, E. *The Six Value Medals*, Vermilion, 2005

Wheatley, M. *Finding Our Way: Leadership for an Uncertain Time*, Berrett-Koehler, 2007

Hailey, J (2000). 'Indicators of Identity: NGOs and the strategic imperative of assessing core values', in *Development in Practice*, Vol. 10, No. 3

Henderson, M and Thompson, D, 'How do values influence group development and organisational culture?'. Article on Values at Work website: www.valuesatwork.org

Chapter 2
Relationships

This chapter looks at the importance of thinking about how relationships are initiated, negotiated, nurtured and maintained. Methods for negotiating and promoting good relationships are suggested. The values and principles underpinning a programme are reflected in how relationships are conducted and the power balances within those relationships.

Values and principles

'Relationships are key to accessing necessary resources and also to the ability to deliver quality service.'
(James Taylor, CDRA)

Establishing relationships

If **'working collaboratively'** and taking an **'empowering'** approach to the work are core values of an organisation, then investing in relationship building will be a significant element of the design and implementation of a capacity building programme. However, relationships take time, energy, self awareness, openness and trust in order to become strong and reliable. This is often overlooked in the design phase of the programming. It is particularly critical to invest in this when establishing a capacity building programme in a new area or region. Sufficient time and resources need to be allocated within the 'start up' phase, so that the key individuals who are implementing the programme are able to explore and identify the common ground which will sustain the relationship once the pressures of the implementation phase kick in.

> **Case example**
>
> Organisation A is starting work in a new region, and has established contact with a number of capacity building providers to support and work with, including a local CSO, a consultancy firm and a professional association. Through a process of discussion, spending time with all three, learning about each organisation's approach to development and its values and principles, it has established which organisation has the best 'value fit' to pursue a capacity building programme with.

Establishing relationships often begins with identifying common ground – for example, shared interests, understanding and world view. A key element is ensuring there is the opportunity to discuss what is important to each of the actors. The challenge lies in creating enough initial trust between the key actors to be able to explore core values and principles openly and explicitly, as well as what is implied or hidden.

↩ Part Two, Chapter 1

Power within relationships

At the core of establishing, negotiating and maintaining relationships is unequal power between the parties in the relationship. Processes need to be put in place to minimise this power imbalance as experience suggests ignoring it will lead to ineffective relationships and consequently ineffective programmes.

The following questions will help in thinking through the power issue at the design phase:

- Whose interests does this programme serve?
- Is there a direct relationship between the funder and the capacity building provider – what are the power implications?

↩ Part Two, Chapter 3

- How explicit are the power dynamics?

The aid chain

This is the classic view of a top-down aid chain:

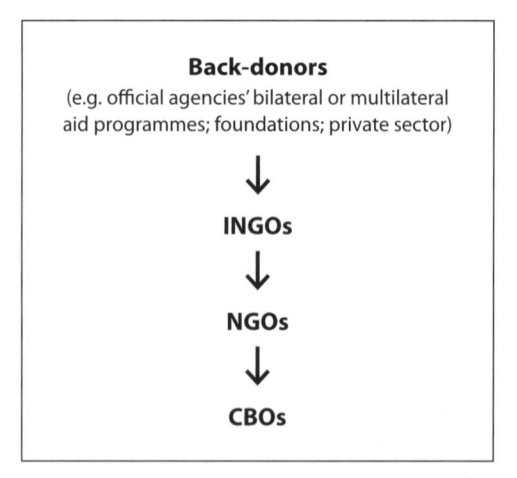

Back-donors
(e.g. official agencies' bilateral or multilateral aid programmes; foundations; private sector)
↓
INGOs
↓
NGOs
↓
CBOs

It is not surprising that the aid chain is a contributing factor to the power imbalance in relationships in development. In its simplest form, financial resources flow from the back donors, like the UN, World Bank, northern or western governments; through bilateral programmes with recipient southern or eastern governments; often filtered via INGOs, who in turn support development programmes with local NGOs who work with and through community based organisations who have the direct contact with the intended beneficiaries.

The last five years has seen shifts in the 'aid architecture', with new actors appearing (e.g. Gates Foundation) and relationships becoming more complex. It may no longer be appropriate to describe the architecture in terms of a linear chain, as there are now different models of funding, including direct funding of local community organisations by bilateral/multilateral donor programmes oriented towards civil society.

Nevertheless, most capacity building programmes take place within a context of hierarchy, whereby the values and principles of the highest are imposed upon the lowest. For example, a results-oriented back donor seeking tangible outcomes may have values that are not shared by a capacity building support provider seeking to ensure an inclusive process which leads to confidence building and ownership of the outcomes by the beneficiaries. Compromises are often made below in the aid chain to accommodate such values from above. There is often little room for negotiating the relationship.

The following steps may be taken in the design and implementation of a capacity building programme to minimise this risk:

1. Be aware of the aid chain and make others in the relationship aware of it. No programme works in a vacuum and the external context can have either a positive or negative impact on programme design.

2. Work to make explicit the agendas behind engaging in this work, by developing explicit policies and definitional reference.

   Part Two, Chapter 7

3. Discuss values and principles underpinning the programme design with stakeholders so that they can be negotiated and shared openly before the programme implementation. (This includes back donors as well as potential partners/clients.)

4. Have a written statement of principles which can be openly shared.

   Part Two, Chapter 4

5. Check whose interests the capacity building programme serves.

6. Ensure that there are channels of communication so that learning and capacity building takes place up and down the chain

An awareness and understanding of the institutional web of power relations will assist in an analysis of the donor agendas, geo-political dynamics and relationships along the aid chain. By maintaining this awareness, capacity building support providers will be better able to locate some of the underlying agendas that are informing donor approaches to initiatives and respond in a more informed manner.

   Part Two, Chapter 7

Power and partnerships in capacity building

'Partnership' is potentially the main area for values and principles to be absorbed into rhetoric. Most organisations refer to partnerships not relationships, implying a more established, more meaningful and deeper type of liaison. However, partnership is often an overly used and misused term – for many it is almost synonymous with capacity building. The values and principles espoused in partnership working are often devalued because assumptions are made about what these values mean in practice and inherent power imbalances are not openly discussed and addressed.

For example, a capacity building partnership based on a value of 'shared responsibility' – does it imply shared responsibility for the outcomes of the capacity building initiative, for fundraising for it, or for shared governance?

It may be useful to explicitly analyse the degree of power that is to be attributed to the actors in the capacity building relationship. One framework that can help is Fowler's 'depths of engagement' model, adapted for capacity building programming. There are four depths of relationships, each related to the level of participation of both parties. Following participation principles, relational depth can be conceived as a scale of influence that can be negotiated. The four depths of engagement are:

> Information exchange > Consultation > Shared influence > Joint control

Information exchange is at the 'shallow' end of the engagement, and joint control at the 'deep' end.

> **Examples of the four depths of engagement in capacity building initiatives:**
>
> **Information exchange**: An organisation implementing a capacity building programme may inform local CSOs of the opportunities open to them with regard to their participation in the various capacity building initiatives taking place. The activities may include open training courses; grant schemes; roundtable discussions etc. These are defined and implemented by the capacity building provider and there is no obligation to wait for, or be tied to, a response by the CSOs to the information provided.
>
> **Consultation**: Local CSOs are invited to provide feedback on the potential content of a capacity building programme. They may participate in a needs assessment exercise, but there is no expectation that they will engage in the decision making process. Their views may be sought during the implementation of the initiative, leading to subsequent adjustments and review of the initial design.
>
> **Shared influence**: Local CSOs are engaged in shaping the programme, providing ideas and opinions on the different elements. They will be involved in decision making about appropriate methods and may also contribute to the design of specific tools.
>
> **Joint control**: Local CSOs are full members of the programme management committee. Together with the programme sponsors and implementers, they are engaged in decision making at all levels – on the objectives, strategies, activities and resourcing of the initiative.

There are different rights and obligations involved with each of these depths, which will need to be explicitly discussed and negotiated if the relationship between capacity building sponsor/implementer and participating CSO is to be healthy and transparent (see next section).

> **? Critical thoughts**
>
> Are you clear on the level of engagement you are working with in your capacity building programme?
>
> Have you clearly expressed this to other stakeholders?

Finally, if you are engaged in partner capacity building work then your organisation's approach to partnership will influence that work. So, for example, an INGO developing a partner capacity building programme might operate with an approach to partnership that is determined by its own organisation-wide strategic objectives. The INGO will choose partners according to the objectives it is working towards during any specific strategic period. If these objectives change then the capacity building work will be affected, as the partner will no longer be of interest to the INGO if they don't work in the same programme area as the new strategic objectives.

The question will be – is this explicit in the relationship? Do the partners know that their involvement in the capacity building programme will be determined by their degree of fit with the INGO's overall objectives?

Part Three, Chapter 6

Negotiating relationships in capacity building

A healthy relationship is characterised by an agreed level of mutuality and balance in terms of the **rights and obligations** of the parties involved. Negotiating and agreeing these may form a core part of establishing clarity and transparency for the capacity building initiative.

Being aware of the cultural and contextual setting will help in the negotiation of the relationship. Terms of Reference or Memorandum of Understanding are a useful starting point in working towards an agreed mandate for working together. Negotiating is a skill, laden with issues of power – how a relationship is negotiated depends upon the power dynamics between parties. For example, often, the donor assumes power and the recipient of funds accepts that assumption, as challenging it may result in withdrawal of funding. However, if values are openly established and Terms of Reference agreed upon, then this provides a framework within which to negotiate more equally.

Relationships may be less effective because there is a hidden or open mismatch between what each party considers their rights when compared with obligations the other organisation feels towards them. Relationships can flounder when there is a lack of clarity. Issues of power and values are fundamental in this type of negotiation process.

A rights and obligations approach to negotiation makes essential relational issues transparent. It illuminates differences in assumptions, needs and sensitivities so that they can be discussed instead of being avoided.

> **? Critical thoughts**
>
> What rights and obligations do you think all parties have within your capacity building programme?
>
> How can you share this openly between all parties? How open are you to others' points of views?
>
> How will you negotiate a clear and transparent relational framework?

Maintaining relationships

A relationship established and negotiated appropriately has firm foundations upon which it can be maintained. It is important to regularly revisit values and principles, to monitor the relationship and keep it on track. Breakdown can occur when values and principles, once shared, are no longer, and when the parties forget to check that assumptions, even explicit agreements made at the beginning, are still valid for both. Steps in maintaining relationships include:

1. Create regular opportunities to discuss the relationships as part of the monitoring system.

2. Ensure values and principles are visible, through documents, website, office wall etc.

3. Ensure that new stakeholders (e.g. new staff, CBOs, CSOs, donors) are made aware of the values and principles underpinning the relationships and programme.

4. Have an agreed checklist of questions that all stakeholders are aware of and can periodically review. For example:

    Are the values and principles we shared at the beginning still valid – how are they expressed in practice?

    What observations have you made about the power dynamics – is there an imbalance? How are power issues expressed in our relationship?

    What do you value about the relationship and why?

    How could the relationship be improved?

5. Include values and principles of the relationship as process indicators for the capacity building programme.

6. Create opportunities for celebrating the progress of the relationship – success stories, valuing people, learning milestones, positive change etc.

7. Agree a process for if communications and relationships break down. This might include bringing in an independent third party to mediate in any dispute.

> **? Critical thoughts**
>
> When did you last have a purposeful discussion about the organisational values and principles that underpin your capacity building work, both within your own organisation and with partners and clients?
>
> Are assumptions being made because opportunities for explicit dialogue are sidetracked or not given value? What does that say about the underlying and hidden values?
>
> What steps can you take to provide opportunities, encourage discussion and make necessary changes?

SUMMARY

Relationships take time, energy, self awareness, openness and trust in order to become strong and reliable, and this area is often overlooked in the design phase of the programming. Key points include:

- Those moving into a new area and new relationships must factor in additional start-up investment costs.
- Measures need to be put in place to minimise the power imbalance – ignoring it will lead to ineffective relationships and ineffective programmes.
- An awareness and understanding of the institutional web of power relations will assist in an analysis of the aid architecture. By undertaking this analysis, capacity building support providers will be better able to locate some of the underlying agendas that are informing donor approaches to initiatives and respond in a more informed manner.
- The values and principles expressed in partnership working are often devalued because assumptions are made about what these values mean in practice and inherent power imbalances are not openly discussed and addressed.
- A healthy relationship is characterised by mutuality and balance, agreed in terms of the **rights and obligations** of the parties involved. Negotiating and agreeing these may form a core part of establishing **clarity** and **transparency** for the capacity building initiative.

RECOMMENDED READING

Brehm, V. *Promoting Effective North-South NGO Partnerships*. INTRAC, 2001

Brehm, V et al. *Autonomy or Dependence? Case Studies of North-South NGO Partnerships*. INTRAC, 2004

Fowler, A. *Partnerships: Negotiating Relationships – a resource for NGDOs*. INTRAC, 2000

Chapter 3
Values and principles expressed in organisational policies

Values and principles

An organisation's underlying values and principles shape its culture and identity, and are expressed in its overarching policies. Equally, specific capacity building initiatives may express values and principles that have implications for the organisation at large. This chapter aims to explore the relationship between organisational policies and the design and implementation of capacity building work. To illustrate, two common organisational policies, mainstreaming HIV/AIDS and gender, are explored with reference to their implications for capacity building programming and implementation.

Existing organisational policies

Organisational policies should be the expression of an organisation's inner values. Policies guide practice and are therefore important when considering designing a capacity building programme. It is important to take stock of what policies already exist (and what policies are absent that perhaps should exist) and their implications for the programme design. Policies may be found in all three organisational dimensions:

Internal dimension: For example, staff welfare policies, learning and education opportunities, equal opportunities policies, staff development, reward systems etc.

Programme dimension: For example, mainstreaming policies such as gender and disabilities; conflict prevention policies etc.

Relational dimension: For example, partnership policies; policies to guide supporter recruitment; donor relation policies etc.

Designing the capacity building programme should include an internal review of:

- What policies exist, and what is their potential relevance to the capacity building work?
- What values underpin that policy?
- Can or should these values be reflected in the capacity building programme?
- If so, how can this be done and what are the implications for the programme?
- If specific policies do not exist that are important to the programme, what can be done?

> **Case example**
>
> Organisation Z has a new gender mainstreaming policy and the managers of the capacity building programmes are considering the implications of this. For example, they are looking at what it means to apply a gender perspective to decisions about the scope of the initiative, the nature of the strategies and activities etc. In sum, they are recognising that the overarching 'capacity for what?' question needs to add: 'and what are the gender implications?'.

HIV/AIDS policy and capacity building programming

HIV/AIDS has had an enormous impact on international development efforts. Its ubiquitous nature means that development organisations cannot ignore it and be without either a specific policy or general health guidelines. In contexts of high prevalence, it may be more appropriate to think of capacity *maintenance* rather than capacity *development*. The implications for capacity building programming exist at different levels:

- **Organisational level**

- Can your organisation offer guidance and support?
- Does it have a policy of mainstreaming HIV/AIDS awareness?
- What are the implications for the programme?
- How should some of the principles be applied to the programme level – are they appropriate to the context?

- **Donor level**

- Do potential donors of the programme have such policies in place?
- If so, what are the implications for the design and implementation of the capacity building programme?
- If they don't then what are the implications for the programme? How can you influence them?

- **Programme level – capacity building design and implementation**

- Does the contextual analysis of how HIV/AIDS affects primary stakeholders and beneficiaries of the programme (for example programme staff, and at community, organisational, partner level) indicate a need for a policy to be in place?
- What are the implications of having a policy for non-discriminatory practice, financial support and health care provision for programme staff?
- In contexts of high prevalence there may be a capacity *reduction*. Is your analysis and design of capacity building initiatives taking this into consideration?
- Do your potential partners have policies in place – how will this affect the design of your programme?

- Who should be involved in the development of the programme design and implementation?
- How can the programme objectives reinforce the need to be aware of the impact of HIV/AIDS on organisational and sector wide capacity?
- Be aware of how the delivery of capacity building activities may be affected by, for example the fact that HIV/AIDS affected people may not be able to consistently attend all events; the timing of activities might need to take into account people's family commitments because of increased need; the pace may need to be adjusted because of energy levels.
- When setting objectives and identifying the key capacity building strategies, it may be necessary to consider: building awareness of how HIV/AIDS impacts on organisational capacity, promoting internal HIV/AIDS policies, and facilitating the sharing of best practice of CSOs who have worked with such policies.

The following extract illustrates policy development by Dutch INGOs with regard to their work with partners, and to supporting partner capacity development.

Case example

The first objective in having guidelines is connected to achieving the idea of **'good donorship'**. The guidelines are part of a process of us becoming better donors in the context of HIV/AIDS. In order to produce them we have been through a process of developing and deciding upon our position with regard to our partners, their workplace policies, and our responsibilities. This leads to a second objective concerning **managing HIV/AIDS in the workplace**: that by clarifying and communicating our position, along with the country level support we are providing, we hope to assist our partners in their efforts to develop and implement their own workplace policies. All of this leads to an **overarching aim**, of supporting our partners to reduce the impacts which HIV/AIDS has on their work, and so to protect their performance and effectiveness.

The **values-based reasons** are to do with being a socially responsible employer, or one which meets its moral obligations to attend to its employees' well-being. They are also grounded in rights; if we as donor organisations believe that everyone should have the right to health care, we should do what we can to help partners to secure that right for their employees.

Extract of Principles

a) We believe that all donors should fund a share of their partners' overheads, including the cost of workplace policies, in addition to funding projects or activities.

b) We recognize that the impacts of HIV/AIDS can cause partners to produce lower levels of outputs for the same investment.

c) We believe that the cost of inaction is greater than the cost of action to manage the impacts of HIV/AIDS. Workplace policies are a cost-effective method which all organisations can use to reduce the impacts of HIV/AIDS on their work.

d) We note that, as autonomous organisations, partners are responsible for developing, implementing, monitoring, and evaluating their own workplace policies. However, we will support them as set out by our commitments in these guidelines.

e) We believe that donors and partners need to communicate openly about the challenges brought about by HIV/AIDS, and are committed to doing so.

f) We recognize that partners need to create workplace policies to fit their context, if they are to have effective policies which they can keep up.

g) Partners must decide who to include in their workplace policies. We expect that their policies will attend to gender issues, and that they will not discriminate between different cadres of employees. We also prefer that direct family members are covered including, where relevant, access to antiretroviral treatment.

h) We commit to following the ILO key principles in our workplace policies, and expect that partners will also be guided by them.

i) We are not, in the pilot projects, making funding conditional upon partners demonstrating that they are actively trying to manage HIV/AIDS in their workplaces. We will, however, adjust our own grant assessment processes to include attention to the issue, and will favourably view an organisation's efforts to manage the risks that HIV/AIDS presents to its work.

...

k) We undertake to provide technical, and sometimes financial, support to partners through the pilot projects as they develop their workplace policies.

l) We want partners to integrate their workplace policies within their overall budgets, to form part of their ordinary applications for three years' funding. We will positively consider all such applications as part of usual assessment procedures, including funding our share of the costs of prevention, care, support, and treatment. We expect that the net costs of workplace policies will be up to about 4% of the total payroll (salaries plus benefits).

...

o) We commit to advocating good donorship among the wider community of donor agencies, with the aim of increasing the proportion of donors who are willing to support partners' efforts to manage HIV/AIDS through workplace policies. We expect that partners will also engage in advocacy to influence their donors.

...

q) We undertake to monitor and evaluate the process and outcomes of the pilot projects, and expect to be held accountable to the commitments that we have made to good donorship in these guidelines.

Source: Good Donorship in a time of AIDS, developed by Cordaid, Hivos, ICCO and Novib - who, with the Dutch AIDS Fund, form the collaborative organisation STOP AIDS NOW! March, researched and written by Sue Holden.

> **? Critical thoughts**
>
> Do you or your partners have a HIV/AIDS policy? What are the principles underlying such a policy, or the absence of one?
>
> How will this affect the design of the capacity building programme and its implementation?
>
> Could developing such a policy be a component of the capacity building programme itself?

Gender and capacity building programming

The mainstreaming of gender is high on the agenda of many development organisations. Looking at the work of capacity building through a 'gender sensitive lens' implies an understanding that gender issues permeate throughout all levels of capacity building, from societal to individual. It also implies that 'capacity' can be analysed through this lens. As seen earlier, the idea of capacity to do or be means having the *power* as well as the *ability* to do or be something. Working with capacity issues involves dealing with issues of power dynamics and this in turn, means addressing issues of gender relations and power.

↔ Part One, Chapter 1

> **? Critical thoughts**
>
> Does your organisation have a gender mainstreaming policy? Have you considered the implications for the design and implementation of the capacity building programme?
>
> If your organisation does not have a policy in place, how can you ensure that gender mainstreaming is an integral part of your programme and how can it influence the development of policy change in your organisation?

The following gender dimensions should be considered when designing a capacity building initiative:

- **Gender sensitive lens**

At each phase of design and implementation consideration of gender should be cross cutting. Use the lens sensitively, clarifying assumptions and negotiating a method for introducing gender into the design and implementation of the capacity building process.

> Example: when carrying out a contextual scan questions about gender need to be included. If potential partners are unaware of gender issues, this should become an element in the design and an area for capacity building in the implementation phase.

- **Negotiate introduction of gender**

Use the design phase to negotiate issues and concepts about gender. If men and women are not appropriately represented then discuss how this can be initiated and phased into a programme.

> Example: the contextual analysis has highlighted that presently only men are represented at senior level in potential partner organisations, meaning this will affect who is involved in the design and implementation of the programme. Negotiation may include opening up the programme to other levels within the organisation, including other partner organisations with women represented at senior level, looking at recruitment and selection processes etc.

- **Time frame**

Will including gender affect the timescale? Bringing in new elements may involve increasing time in analysis, design and implementing the programme. It may involve greater preparation time before the program begins. How does this affect funding timelines?

- **Women: Dual roles**

Is there an understanding of women's dual role and responsibilities at individual to societal level and how does this affect their participation in a capacity building programme? How can the programme be designed to accommodate such needs in a sensitive way?

- **Selection of participants**

If participants for the programme are to be selected are those undertaking the selection gender aware? Does some work need to be done to ensure this, for example criteria and guidelines established?

- **Discussion of gender dimension within civil society in general**

Is there space in the programme to discuss issues of gender at societal level to ensure that a holistic approach is taken to gender awareness? What aspects of civil society hinder gender relations and equality and how can the programme realistically address these issues?

Values implicit in gender mainstreaming

Consideration should be given to the values implicit in gender mainstreaming. The following questions may be helpful:

- What are the values underpinning gender mainstreaming?
- Do I share and act upon these values – what evidence is there of this?
- Do other stakeholders in the programme share these values or hold other values – is there a mismatch and how can we come closer in our understanding?
- What role do I and others have in promoting gender mainstreaming?
- Do I and others have the space, time and resources to gender mainstream?
- What action do we need to take to ensure gender mainstreaming in our programming?

SUMMARY

Implicit in organisational policies are underlying values and principles that form part of the culture and identity of an organisation. These values are not exclusive to the policy and have implications for programmatic working. Capacity building programming may also have values and principles that have implications for the organisation at large, and for other stakeholders such as partner organisations, donors, beneficiaries and so on.

Organisational policies can be viewed as the expression of an organisation's inner values. Policies guide practice and are therefore important when considering designing a capacity building programme. It is important to take stock of what policies already exist and the implications for the programme design.

RECOMMENDED READING

Porter, F and Sweetman, C (eds). *Mainstreaming Gender in Development: A Critical Review*. Oxfam, 2005

www.eldis.org/gender

www.bridge.ids.ac.uk

Holden, S. *AIDS on the Agenda: Adapting Development and Humanitarian Programmes to Meet the Challenge of HIV/AIDS*. Oxfam, 2003

ACORD. *Good Practices for Challenging Stigma and Discrimination and Rights Promotion of People living with HIV/AIDS*. 2007

James, R. *Building Organisational Resilience to HIV/AIDS: Implications for Capacity Building*. INTRAC, 2005

Chapter 4
Statement of principles for capacity building programming

This chapter introduces the importance and potential benefits of working with a statement of principles that reflect the values of a particular organisation or capacity building programme. Continuing exploring why values and principles are important in the design and implementation of the programme, this chapter helps the reader to think through how to make explicit a sometimes difficult and intangible area for discussion between stakeholders so that these values can more easily and openly guide the programme work.

Values and principles

> **Critical thoughts**
>
> Is your organisation prepared to make explicit the values and principles influencing its capacity building work?
>
> What are the implications in doing so for you, your organisation and your partners or clients?

Why a statement of principles?

A statement of capacity building principles is a public declaration of the values that influence actions, behaviours and decisions in the capacity building work of an organisation. The statement may draw on known generic good practice principles in addition to the organisation's own core values. It may be a mix of values that are known to be put into practice already, together with some more aspirational values.

Producing a statement of capacity building principles means that the organisation is prepared to be held publicly accountable for how it carries out its capacity building practice, as well as for the results it achieves. It can facilitate the organisational learning and understanding about the fit between what it aspires to do and the reality of its behaviour. It also implies that the organisation wishes to promote its approach to this work as being values-driven.

Part One, Chapter 4

Starting the process

For a statement of principles to have meaning and ownership, the process of deciding upon that statement needs to be inclusive and grounded in reality. Words can be interpreted in different ways, for example, 'cooperation' may mean different things to different people. So a set of words is not enough for principles to be understood, accepted, and used in practice. Getting started on a statement of principles requires resource commitment in terms of time and staff.

The **key steps** in the process of developing a statement of principles are:

- Being clear about why a statement of principles is important
- Gaining leadership commitment
- Having a driver for change and to lead the process
- Getting managers and staff on board
- Taking stock – where are we at in terms of core values reflected in our work?
- Gathering evidence – what already exists – documents, statements, materials?
- Sharing knowledge and experience – what values cannot be negotiated?
- Holding a focused workshop – what does quality capacity building practice mean for us and our work?
- Sharing the outcomes and consulting with a wider group of external stakeholders
- Taking stock – what are the implications for operationalising quality practice?
- Addressing any issues or concerns
- Drafting a statement – consulting internal and external stakeholders
- Piloting a statement – in different contexts, cultures and clients
- Getting feedback and learning from the process
- Reviewing and adjusting
- Developing a monitoring system to help with continuous learning.

> **◉ Case example: Towards a statement of principles**
>
> **Stage 1 – Going back to why**
>
> We asked 'why is a statement of principles important to us?' We already had a statement about our core values that underpins our vision and mission and we wanted to carry these values into our capacity building work, especially as capacity building is our core business.
>
> **Stage 2 – Starting the process**
>
> Staff agreed that this was important and would help with our own internal capacity building and learning. A member of the leadership team took responsibility and oversaw the process The first task was to source references to 'values and principles in practice', for example, in our training materials and publications. This formed a reference for future discussions.

Stage 3 – Finding out what already works in practice

We discussed with staff some of our **core values that already implicitly affect the way we work**. We then discussed the elements of our core values that needed to be reflected in our capacity building work.

Stage 4 – Linking to the issue of quality

We had been engaged with other capacity building practitioners in debates on this subject. These discussions enabled us to make the connection between 'quality capacity building' work, and work that is shaped by our values. We held an internal workshop which discussed **indicators of quality practice**. We clustered these into:

1. Process
2. Outcomes and impact of capacity building work
3. Individual facilitator/change agent

Stage 5 – Sharing the process and outcomes

We then shared the outcomes so far with a **broader internal stakeholder group**, including board members and associates. It became clearer that the indicators of quality capacity building were actually our 'capacity building principles'. We then formulated these principles into a draft public statement, which was shared with external stakeholders.

Stage 6 – Where are we now?

We are thinking through how to operationalise these principles. There are certain **implications**, for example:

- **Staff competencies**: what skills, knowledge, behaviours, and personal values are required?
- **Monitoring**: how do you monitor such an approach, e.g. incorporating it into the monitoring of staff performance?
- **Systems**: do we have the appropriate systems in place and how do we, for example, formalise the use of the statement in contractual relationships?
- **Accountability**: who is accountable to whom? How can we get our clients or donors on board?
- **Identity**: we need to continue asking our clients 'what do you value about us?' This will inform and reinforce what is important to others in terms of what is valued by them.
- **Continuous learning**: we wish to learn from others' experience in this kind of approach. This could be achieved by creating a pool of examples of existing Codes of Capacity Building Practice and Statements of Principles, identifying and promoting the benefits, sharing learning etc.

Source: INTRAC, 2006

> **? Critical thoughts**
>
> Is there the political will to commit to developing a statement of principles in your organisation?
>
> Where are the drivers for change and how can they work together to begin the process?
>
> What leaders need to be convinced about the benefits of a proposal?
>
> Who might block the process and how can you win them over?

The principles

There are different ways of expressing these. Some organisations prefer brief one page documents, others prefer to add more detailed text. Some will include them in their core organisational documents, whilst others will produce stand-alone statements. Each organisation should identify the most appropriate manner in which it wishes to express these principles. It may be useful to consider the different categories of principles – those involved with process; outcomes and impact; and those related to the individuals involved in the capacity building work. The headline principles developed in the case study above lead to a statement that contained the following:

> **Case example: Extracts from a public statement of capacity building principles**
>
> INTRAC aspires to engage in a practice which reflects the following:
>
> **a) Process**
>
> A first group of principles are those related to the actual intervention (the 'what', 'how', 'when' of the process):
>
> **Values driven:** the approach is informed by a value-set shaped around social justice, equity, well-being, empowerment, with a core belief in the critical contribution to societal change made by civil society organisations. Consideration is made of the role that values play in influencing the motivations, design, implementation and outcomes of the process. Efforts will be taken to make explicit the values-base of the actors involved, of the organisation as a whole and of other influencing environmental forces.
>
> **Power aware and power challenging:** recognising that power dynamics are at play during the process and seeking to make these explicit wherever appropriate. The practitioner will be aware of how their own power is influencing the process, and will seek to make this explicit and negotiable.
>
> **Gender aware:** awareness of how gender relations play out within the process as well as how they shape the overall context of the intervention. Aspiring to incorporate a gender dimension in all phases of the action-reflection cycle.
>
> **Client-centred:** processes are self-generated and owned by the clients. We recognise that this is not always how initiatives start, but we will seek to ensure that once we are involved, the processes engage with this principle.

Holistic: retaining focus whilst taking into account the whole picture of the client, and the contextual factors influencing it and which it wishes to influence.

Funding-detached: quality practice is more likely to occur when it is completely delinked from any broader resourcing decisions to be made about that client. Therefore, INTRAC will not engage in grant funding initiatives, or in providing services that are imposed on clients as funding conditions.

Reflective and researched: seeking to ground the design, implementation and learning in quality diagnosis of the client's experiences and practice. We believe that a reflective practice will work with monitoring and evaluation methods and systems that are appropriate to the scale, scope and purpose of the initiative.

Contextually appropriate: capacity building services must be grounded in the specific cultural, political, organisational context within which it is implemented. However, there is scope for introducing elements from outside the immediate context – in an appropriate, sensitive and flexible manner. We believe that in a global world, knowledge and learning should not be concentrated within any particular locality. So long as the client can take the lead and decide how far they wish to engage in this process of exchange, we would consider this an appropriate approach.

Adaptive: INTRAC does not work with pre-prepared 'packages' of interventions. We combine different elements in different ways, with approaches adapted in an appropriate manner to the client, purpose and context.

Developmental: both within the client system; and within the 'supply' system by working to strengthen the further development of local support capacity.

Practical and pragmatic: we seek to achieve what we believe in, but are prepared to start with where the client is.

Timely and cost effective: appropriate pacing of interventions, scale and scope.

b) Outcome and impact

It is important to have some quality indicators for the effects of our work with clients, at the level of their organisational capacity as well as for the longer term impact on the external environment.

Relevant and appropriate: we seek changes in the client that will contribute to the objectives, as measured against indicators established by the client.

Producing societal change: aim to contribute towards achieving an impact in the world. We would aspire to this impact being related to achieving a shift in power balances in favour of the poor, marginalised, discriminated, voiceless etc.

Non-deterministic: openness to recognise unexpected results.

c) The facilitator or change agent

INTRAC believes that the individual practitioner brings themselves into the capacity building process and that how we are in our practice will affect the quality of that practice. 'Integrity' is the key personal quality of the facilitator. Facilitators bring intuition, wisdom, experience and judgement as they engage with this ever-shifting terrain. Self-knowledge and humility are also key characteristics, as are flexibility and the ability to use a range of different intervention styles.

Source: INTRAC, 2006

SUMMARY

This chapter covers the importance and potential benefits of working with a statement of principles that reflect the values of a particular organisation or capacity building programme.

Producing a statement of capacity building principles means that the organisation is prepared to be held accountable for the way it carries out its capacity building practice, as well as for the results it achieves. It can facilitate the organisational learning and understanding about the fit between what it aspires to do and the reality of its behaviour. It also implies that the organisation wishes to promote its approach to this work as being values-driven.

RECOMMENDED READING

An example of a Code of Ethics for Organisational Development practitioners can be found at: www.odinstitute.org/ethics.htm

Chapter 5
Learning and change

For a culture of learning to flourish, certain values and beliefs need to be in place. This chapter looks at factors which enable or inhibit organisational learning and implications for the design and implementation of capacity building programming. It explores the values and principles that promote organisational learning, and develop and sustain a culture of learning. In particular, it highlights the importance of double loop learning as a central concept to successful capacity building. Capacity building needs to be a two-way process whereby the capacity building provider is also part of the learning process, which leads to changes within their own organisation as well as that of capacity building partners or civil society organisations. Learning is a value and principle in itself and permeates throughout an organisation. In relation to the body framework, **'two-way learning'** runs along the whole length of the spine. This chapter explores how such a value becomes an innate principle of capacity building.

Values and principles

⟷ Part Three, Chapter 8

Factors which enable learning

A learning culture within an organisation does not exist without being nurtured by leaders and staff. This culture is underpinned by a set of organisational values which value learning itself. For this, certain factors need to be in place:

1. Developing and sustaining a culture supportive of learning (see page 68)
2. Being open to reflection and change – open to double loop learning, reflecting on action and making necessary changes (see table on page 69)
3. Learning needs to be explicit and legitimised by providing time and space for learning opportunities (see table on page 71)

> **? Critical thought**
> Are these factors present in your organisation?

1. Developing and sustaining a culture supportive of learning

The box below indicates the factors that need to be in place for a learning culture to thrive. The overriding concern is that learning must be legitimised within the organisation. This approach is critical to double loop learning.

An organisational culture supportive of learning

An organisational culture supportive of learning is one that enables, encourages, values, rewards and uses the learning of its members both individually and collectively. NGOs with a learning culture demonstrate that:

- learning is a **legitimate activity.** Learning is seen as an integral part of each individual's work responsibilities, not something to be done in the individual's own time.
- learning is **encouraged and supported.** Managers make it their responsibility to ensure that their colleagues are given personal encouragement to contribute to the development of the organisation's practice and policy.
- learning is given **adequate resources.** There is a recognition that learning takes time and it may also require other resources, including funding.
- learning is **rewarded.** Mechanisms for rewarding, valuing and acknowledging organisational learning act as a significant incentive for staff to invest time and resources in learning at both organisational and individual levels. These can include: building learning responsibilities into job descriptions; acknowledging contribution throughout the year and not only at annual performance appraisals; ensuring that learning is seen as enhancing career prospects.
- the organisation aims to **overcome its internal barriers** to learning. Strategies for addressing internal barriers to learning, based on a systematic analysis, are devised and made clear to all members of the organisation.

Source: Bruce Britton, 'Organisational Learning in NGOs', Praxis Paper 3, INTRAC, March 2005.

Values and principles promoting learning

An organisational culture that supports learning will hold the following core values and principles:

- Staff member's ideas, concerns, feelings and knowledge are valued.
- Active listening – what staff have to say and do is valued.
- Constructive feedback – mistakes are used as learning opportunities, challenges and differences of opinion are viewed as healthy for the organisation.
- No blame culture – there is collective responsibility, where learning takes place at all levels – team, organisation and programmes.
- Innovation and creativity – provide opportunities for new initiatives and continuous improvement.
- Learning is an organisational goal – leadership recognises and prioritises learning as an expected aspect of good practice.

> **Case example: CAFOD and Christian Aid – Learning Culture**
>
> By identifying those people who were supportive of organisational learning and interested to find out more no matter where they were located in the organisation, CAFOD was able to build a critical mass of support for a wide range of organisational learning initiatives, starting with the organisation's opinion leaders. Christian Aid identified those with a passionate interest in organisational learning and created a cadre of 'Corporate Revolutionaries' who are located at different levels and locations in the organisation.

> **Critical thought**
>
> In what ways can you tap into different initiatives about the way the organisation learns and changes – how will it inform the design and implementation of a capacity building programme?

2. Openness to reflect and change

If there is a supportive environment for learning then being open to reflection and change will in some cases require changing organisational attitudes to change itself. The concept of action–reflection is a well known method for instilling learning as part of the regular process of monitoring and general work practices. It is harder to make the space and time for reflection, whereas action, particularly for civil society organisations, is a natural process and one that is valued above reflection. However, for learning and change to take place both must be equally valued. The following table illustrates a way of reflecting on learning that can change how organisations behave. The concept of double loop learning is particularly helpful as it assists individuals and organisations to be more challenging and open to change rather than accepting things as they are.

The characteristics of single, double and triple loop learning

	Single Loop Learning	**Double Loop Learning**	**Triple Loop Learning**
Involves	Applying existing rules/procedures	Querying assumptions and rules/procedures	Examining core values and identity
	Dealing with symptoms of problems	Examining underlying causes of problems	Rethinking fundamental purpose and principles
	Thinking 'inside the box'	Thinking 'outside the box'	Thinking 'about the box'
Intended outcomes	More efficient ways of working	More effective ways of working	Renewed statement of core values and purpose
	Improved application of rules/procedures	Improved rules and procedures	Renewed identity
		Improved systems and strategies	
		New knowledge and insights	

A 2006 survey of INGO approaches to capacity building provided an opportunity for respondents to indicate what they had learnt about themselves and their capacity whilst being engaged in such work. Forty-four organisations answered this question, and below is a short summary of these.

> More than a third explicitly indicated in their responses that they saw capacity building as two-way. Typical responses included: 'We always learn more about ourselves from these engagements – both our capabilities and our limitations.' Some emphasised how they had learnt that learning itself is important, which means investing in time for learning and being open to changing approaches and concepts.
>
> Nearly half wrote about the 'safe' ground of learning about programme work in general, and capacity building programming specifically. This included several references to the difficult, high-risk and experimental nature of the work. Some referred to the challenge of tailoring the responses, and of juggling the need to do that with the desire to achieve efficiency through more standardised approaches.
>
> The minority of responses which referred to learning more about themselves and their own capacities gave a mix of examples. Some referred to learning about the leadership of their organisations, others about ensuring they have the right 'people mix' and of the importance of these people being willing to change. Some responses referred to learning about the nature of relationships and the need to invest in new types of relationships, with some specifically mentioning power issues. One went into this in some depth, and included a reference to how working with an '"in the know" perspective can defeat the core empowerment objective'. This respondent referred also to an 'INGO corporate brand which can … envelop civil society in a new form of patron–client relationship'.
>
> Source: 'Taking Stock – a snapshot of INGO engagement in civil society capacity building', B Lipson and H Warren, INTRAC, 2006

3. Creating the space for learning

If the motivation and means for learning are established, then creating the space for learning will ensure opportunities are legitimised and explicit. Creating space involves:

- raising the profile of learning and making it a strategic goal
- integrating learning into the planning, monitoring and evaluation cycle
- investing in knowledge and learning management within an organisation
- building relationships based on trust and openness to enable stakeholders involved in capacity building work to reflect and change.

The next table illustrates examples of how to create space for learning within organisations, which may be adapted to capacity building programming.

Creating the space for learning

	Individual	**Collective**
Formal	Organisations can: - Legitimise learning by building it into job descriptions and appraisals. - Ensure that each person has an individual plan for their learning and development. - Develop 'reflective practitioner' competences. - Set up individual mentoring and coaching schemes. - Enable attendance at training courses and conferences. - Create opportunities for individuals to represent the organisation in networks. - Encourage individuals to publish articles.	Organisations can: - Build learning objectives into programme plans and organisational strategy. - Develop team work as a required way of working. - Develop mechanisms for establishing collective responsibility for results, e.g. create a culture of team work, matrix structure bringing together teams for one-off projects. - Set up action learning sets, learning groups and communities of practice. - Introduce 'no-travel' and 'reflection' periods. - Commission learning reviews to examine work themes. - Create cross-functional teams to develop guidelines or policies. - Include an explicit 'lessons learnt' section in all reports.
Informal	Individuals can: - Build in time for reflection each day and at significant stages of pieces of work. - Engage in informal networking. - Use online discussion forums. - Develop habits that support reflective practice (e.g. keep a learning journal).	Organisations can: - Provide physical space that encourages informal networking. - Set up intranets, newsletters or other ways of keeping people informed about each other's work.

Source: Britton, B, 'Organisational Learning in NGOs: Creating the Motive, Means and Opportunity'. INTRAC, 2005, p31

> **Critical thoughts**
>
> Is there a favourable climate for a learning approach in your organisation? Are leaders facilitating such an approach?
>
> Do you have the means to ensure learning is a cultural norm in your capacity building programme?

Factors which inhibit learning

The factors which inhibit learning within an organisation may be more numerous than those which promote it. Many organisations often remain within a single loop approach to learning.

Factors which inhibit learning:

- The value that an organisation and its leadership place on learning – learning is viewed as an unimportant means to improving the performance of the organisation.
- Inability of an organisation to inwardly reflect on its need for learning and change.
- Approach to accountability – i.e. rigid accountability which values results over process. Learning lessons from programmatic work may appear difficult when donors are more interested in results and financial reporting. The drive to achieve planned results can undermine the ability to learn.
- Organisations are under-resourced or overworked, therefore learning is viewed as a luxury not a priority.

Implications for capacity building programme design

1. For organisations to be effective they need to be able and willing to learn from their experiences. Understanding which programme approaches work and in what contexts is at the root of CSOs' effectiveness. Learning should lead to improvements in future programme designs. The principle of double loop learning therefore is all the more important. Capacity building support providers that are able to respond, learn and change are likely to be more effective programmatically.

2. Learning can mean designing innovative new programmes or policies, but also making small improvements to existing programmes. This may mean ensuring learning is integrated into the **monitoring** process. Learning therefore becomes a 'way of life' that all stakeholders are involved in from, for example, beneficiaries gathering their own community data on raising HIV/AIDS awareness, to policy improvements for partner and support provider organisations.

3. Capacity development strategies are based on a process of organisational assessment (OA). Carrying out an organisational self-assessment and then translating the results of the OA into practical plans for capacity building requires the ability to reflect on and learn from the organisation's experience. In this sense, the competences for organisational learning are an essential means to identify and develop civil society organisational capacity.

4. Learning has an important part to play in **building trust** as the humility that underpins an openness to learning also encourages each stakeholder to value and respect the other's experience. The skills of reflection upon which learning is based can also help each organisation to assess carefully and value what each can contribute to the partnership. By valuing organisational learning there is a greater likelihood of building stronger and more balanced partnerships.

SUMMARY

This chapter highlights the following:

- A learning culture within an organisation only exists by being nurtured by leaders and staff. This culture is underpinned by a set of organisational values which value learning.
- Developing and sustaining a culture supportive of learning requires learning to be legitimised, resourced, and monitored, and barriers challenged and overcome.
- The concept of double loop learning is particularly helpful as it helps individuals and organisations to be more challenging and open to change rather than accepting things as they are.
- Creating the space for learning to take place, e.g. raising the profile of learning and making it a strategic goal; integrating learning into the planning, monitoring and evaluation cycle; investing in knowledge and learning management and building relationships based on trust and openness.
- Factors which inhibit learning may be more numerous than those which promote it. Many organisations often remain within a single loop approach to learning.

RECOMMENDED READING

Argyris, C. *On Organizational Learning*. 1992

Britton, B. *Organisational Learning in NGOs*. INTRAC, 2005

Senge, P. *The Fifth Discipline: The Art and Practice of the Learning Organisation*. Doubleday, 1990

Swieringa, J and Wierdsma, A. *Becoming a Learning Organisation: Beyond the Learning Curve*. Addison-Wesley, 1992

Chapter 6
The values and principles of capacity builders

Values and principles

The previous chapters in Part Two have focused on organisational values and principles and how these shape the capacity building programme. This chapter explores how individual's values and principles influence capacity building work.

Individuals may be actively involved in the implementation of capacity building work in many ways. These 'change agents' engage in multiple roles which may be employed at any one time in the design and implementation of a programme. It is important that individuals are reflective and self aware, as well as being adaptable to the culture and context in which they are operating. The individual's awareness of the values and principles that guide their decisions, behaviour and attitudes will be crucial to the success of the capacity building efforts.

⇔ Part Three, Chapter 6

What is a change agent?

A change agent is a person who provides assistance to others in managing the process of change, so that they can learn from the process and manage change more effectively in the future. The change agent may be 'internal', i.e. from within the organisation, network, etc or may be 'external', i.e. someone from outside of that organisational context.

Capacity building programming needs to consider whether change agents are internal, external or both. Any sponsor of a capacity building programme should identify the existing change agents – those individuals who already play a role of stimulating and accompanying capacity development processes.

⇔ Part Three, Chapter 2

It is critical to the success of the programme that there is awareness about taking on a change agent role at any time. This includes:

- the sponsor unconsciously playing the change agent role themselves (e.g. the INGO staff member initiating the programme's design)
- the capacity building programme manager becoming engaged in the activities
- the members of the participating CSOs when they take on a leadership role in any of the capacity building initiatives

as well as the more obvious:

- external capacity building support provider who is facilitating the development process and engaging in delivering the capacity building activities.

Throughout this chapter 'change agent' can refer to any individuals who may, at some point during a programme, assume the role of catalyst, facilitator or accompanier of a change process.

Any individual working with an organisation in a change process will bring with them a set of values that are shaped by their own history, for example, by their gender, cultural identity, belief system, and world view. Making an understanding of these values and principles explicit, (including attitudes to change itself), increases awareness of how they may be influencing the capacity building process.

Change agent roles and styles

The change agent role alters depending on the style, the situation and needs of the change process at different times. However, at all times the change agent will have an overview of the whole process.

> **Critical thoughts**
>
> As someone engaged in designing and implementing a capacity building programme, are you clear about when you may be playing the change agent role?
>
> As a change agent, you need to decide the most appropriate role for each specific capacity building initiative. Does the most appropriate role reflect your values and principles as well as taking into account the needs of the client?
>
> Are you confident and comfortable in this role?

The diagram below shows the different roles available to a change agent:

The change agent's role regarding degree of directive behaviour							
Reflector	Process specialist	Fact finder	Alternative Identifier	Collaborator in problem-solving	Trainer/ educator	Technical expert	Advocate

CLIENT → CONSULTANT

LEVEL OF CONSULTANT ACTIVITY IN PROBLEM-SOLVING

Non-directive ←――――――――――――――――――――→ Directive

| Raises questions for reflection | Observes problem-solving processes and raises issues mirroring feedback | Gathers data and stimulates thinking | Identifies alternatives and resources for client and helps assess consequences | Offers alternatives and participates in decisions | Trains the client and designs learning experiences | Provides information and suggestions for policy or practice decisions | Proposes guidelines, persuades, or directs in the problem-solving process |

Source: Adapted from G. Lippet and R. Lippet: *The Consulting Process in Action*, University Associates, 1979, p.31

This diagram shows a gradation in the degree to which the change agent takes responsibility for resolving the problems encountered. The roles are based on the principle of who is responsible for the change process and the growth of the client or partner. If responsibility rests with the client then the intervention role of the change agent is low; if there is shared responsibility then there is a moderate intervention role for the change agent; and if the change agent has more of the responsibility then it is a high intervention role. Different intervention levels may be more appropriate at different times in the design and implementation of the programme.

> **Case example**
>
> Organisation Y is designing a long-term capacity building programme. In the early design stages, the programme support provider uses a **facilitative** role when discussing the programme design with stakeholders. During the process however, there are occasions when her experience in capacity building requires the provider to take on a more **technical advisor** role, by sharing knowledge and experience. She runs a workshop, together with a staff member of a partner organisation, the preparation and delivery of which requires the support provider to be **teacher, coach and modeller**, in conjunction with using a **facilitative style** in the workshop. Further into the process, when relationships and trust had been established, the provider frequently takes a **reflective observer** role, as ownership of the process and outcomes becomes more firmly established with the client.

In addition to adopting a variety of roles which depend on the situation, the change agent brings a preferred **style** into the process, which reflects a deeper set of values that they may or may not consciously articulate.

> **Case example**
>
> A support provider may place high value on using a facilitative style. This style aims to build an atmosphere of trust, support and personal acceptance in which clients feel free to be themselves. It is informed by a belief that behaviour can be changed by influencing, encouraging change without being directive. The support provider adds energy, summarises, reflects etc. In this way they aim to shape behaviour by 'selectively augmenting behaviours and tendencies'. This style is influenced by a value set that places greater importance on 'self discovery' than 'direction', and encourages ownership by the client of the capacity building process.
>
> The client organisation may, however, see 'clear direction' and 'strong directive leadership' styles as important and necessary factors to achieve change. The possibility is that the staff of that organisation will interpret the service provider's efforts as 'facipulation', a term often used to describe a sense of being manipulated in a facilitative way. They will believe that a decision has already been taken about potential outputs and outcomes regarding desired behavioural changes, because that is what they are familiar with as the organisation's culture reflects the values of strong directive leadership.

THE VALUES AND PRINCIPLES OF CAPACITY BUILDERS

Reading the context and culture, and applying the appropriate mix of roles and styles to the context, are important first steps in understanding the organisation. Explicitly discussing roles and style where there may be a mismatch of expectations will also be of benefit, so that these issues are made clear early on and not once the process has begun.

The first steps in establishing the most appropriate roles and styles are:

- Be aware of your own preferred styles of working as a change agent.
- Understand the context and the culture within which you are working and the expectations about the role and style of the change agent.
- Reflect on your (or your organisation's) approach to capacity building and the 'values fit'

⇔ Part Three, Chapter 6

- Encourage openness and dialogue to gain commitment and agreement about the role of the change agent.

Finally, when deciding on roles, compromise and flexibility is always required. Change agents continuously adapt to the needs of the situation, a skill in itself. Compromise may be necessary when individual values or style are not the most appropriate for the situation. The change agent must also have the confidence to be open with a client about being flexible and compromising, using the process as a learning opportunity.

Values and principles of the change agent

It is possible to explore more deeply the role of the change agent by looking at the values and principles that they may carry, whether consciously or sub-consciously, into the process of designing and implementing a capacity building programme. A framework for exploring power and values offers an opportunity for the reader to personally reflect and help them towards greater self awareness.

Self reflection

An individual's values and principles are shaped by a variety of factors: background, upbringing, cultural heritage and environment, familial norms, societal values. One of the challenges facing change agents is to nurture and **build critical self-reflection** about the choices made during the design of the programme or specific interventions – to reflect on how power dynamics and values may be influencing choices.

For example, some change agents place a great value on reaching 'ideals', and on the importance of clearly identifying how we may attain those ideals. This value-set may express itself in an approach to capacity building which emphasises the importance of identifying and addressing 'capacity gaps' and correcting perceived deficits. It will lead them to design activities in relation to pre-established descriptions of an ideal capacity level. The tangible outcomes may be expressed in terms of improvements against weaknesses.

For other individuals it may be more to do with a belief in the inherent potential that lies within each person and organisation, without knowing the exact nature of that potential. This change agent might focus on releasing latent abilities. The capacity building activities they favour may focus on facilitating processes which enable the organisation to discover for itself how it might define and attain capacities that best match its vision and mission. The tangible outcomes might be expressed in terms of newly emerging strengths, performance against mission etc.

Both approaches are potentially effective, but the success will depend largely on how appropriate they are to the needs and characteristics of the client as well as to the context. It is important for change agents in both cases to be aware of how their choices of capacity building strategies, activities and indicators have been influenced by their underlying beliefs and values. If not, they risk automatically choosing certain approaches to match their personal value-set rather than the needs of the client.

The following self-reflective questions can be used periodically throughout the capacity building process:

1. How have I contributed to the process so far?
2. What skills/qualities/values have helped or hindered the process?
3. Why did I act/react in a particular way – was it appropriate to the situation?
4. What are the power dynamics that I have observed and my role in that?
5. Is there anything that I need to change about my role, style, attitudes and values to help others and myself towards achieving a positive outcome?

It is important to be **sensitive to power relations and values** during engagement with the client or organisation. An external agent will never have a full grasp of the internal dynamics which are shaping how the client is interacting with the service provider. Internal agents may well be part of the problem. The challenge for change agents is to build self-confidence and establish the means to clearly read the underlying power dynamics which will eventually shape the design, implementation and outcomes of any interventions. For example, whether as an external or internal change agent, the manner in which the TOR and methodology are negotiated and finalised will illustrate where formal and non-formal expressions of power and influence are located within an organisation or client.

> **❓ Critical thoughts**
>
> As an external change agent how aware are you of the process of 'agenda setting' – is it transparent and/or communicated to you? Do you have the language and authority as an external service provider to delve into this complex terrain?
>
> As an internal change agent, are you aware of your own power within the process of agenda setting and its implications for the process of capacity building? Do you have too much or too little power?

Being aware of power and values is a continuous process throughout the programme design and implementation, which requires constant processing, through dialogue, and time and opportunities for reflection and monitoring. Each chapter of this book has highlighted issues of values and power, to emphasise the importance of building in explicit space at each stage of the programme.

Methods and tools for understanding values and power

A change agent who is more critically self aware will be better able to understand the power dynamics at play and the values that they may be carrying into the intervention. They may also be able to adapt different approaches and methodologies appropriately to fit the culture and context, rather than rely on those that they inevitably feel most comfortable with. Whilst there is often merit in replicating what works well and learning from practice about what doesn't, having a truly open approach to new interventions relies less on the past and more on future and new possibilities. Some service providers rely on pre-defined packages, others on looser frameworks which can be adjusted according to context and client. There are power issues concerned with any choice of process, methods and tools.

> **? Critical thoughts**
>
> How do you achieve client confidence and trust without projecting a sense of power and influence which comes from the weight of experience?
>
> What options on methods and tools are you making available to the client or organisation?

It is important to embrace new methods and tools to help explore how values and power dynamics play out within the capacity building process. For example, **values inventories** have been designed to facilitate reflection about the matching of organisational values with those values held by individual staff members. Such tools could be adapted to help make explicit the values held by support providers and clients, and to facilitate a dialogue about a potential 'values-fit' or 'values-clash'.

Another example is in the use of a **values and power framework** to carry out 'values and power scanning'. The primary aim of the tool is to enable analysis of levels of awareness of these two areas simultaneously:

- the ways in which the values are being carried into the intervention by all the actors concerned
- the reading those actors have of how power dynamics are expressing themselves.

A series of checklist questions for each of these two dimensions ('carrying' and 'reading') will enable the practitioner to analyse the degree of understanding with which they are currently operating. This can be plotted visually on a chart and attention can then be paid to the weaker areas which need reinforcing.

CAPACITY BUILDING FRAMEWORK

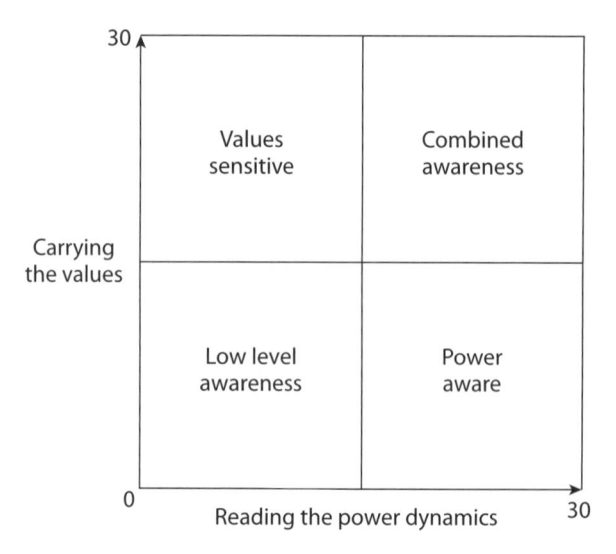

```
30 ↑
         |  Values      | Combined
         |  sensitive   | awareness
Carrying |              |
the values───────────────────────
         |  Low level   | Power
         |  awareness   | aware
         |              |
        0 ─────────────────────→ 30
            Reading the power dynamics
```

Checklist questions:

Score yourself along a grade between 0 and 5 to express the degree to which you agree with each statement (5 being highest agreement). Total the scores for the **values** and the **power** separately and locate yourself in the grid where the two totals meet.

Values:

1. I am fully aware of how this particular capacity building initiative fits within any broader set of values that the (partner/my) organisation might hold.
2. I have full knowledge of the values-based agenda that any organisation financing this initiative it might have (if different from the client organisation).
3. I have identified how my own values might influence this initiative.
4. I have identified how I might mainstream a values-sensitive approach within the design of this initiative.
5. I have a clear strategy for communicating with the (partner/my) organisation about values throughout the intervention.
6. There are agreed indicators within the Terms of Reference for measuring how the intervention will be judged in terms of its value sensitivities.

Power:

1. I am aware of the latest trends in the donor community that may be influencing this initiative.
2. I have had a full and frank dialogue with the (partner/my) organisation about the Terms of Reference, including a joint analysis of the internal dynamics within the organisation which might have influenced the shape and scope of the Terms of Reference.
3. I have discussed openly with the (partner/my) organisation about the consultancy styles that are available and we agree about which one/s to use and why.

4. I have identified what tools, frameworks etc might help me in analysing how my position of power/powerlessness might be influencing my design and implementation choices and behaviour.
5. I have identified how I can keep a constant dialogue with the (partner/my) organisation about the power dynamics that may emerge throughout the intervention.
6. There are agreed indicators within the Terms of Reference for measuring how the intervention will be judged in terms of maintaining an awareness of, and responding positively to, the issues of power relations.

> **Critical thoughts**
>
> Can you identify ways in which the use of such self-awareness tools can be used and discussed openly with colleagues and clients?
>
> Have you consciously reflected on these questions? How can you make time, so that you do not make assumptions about your and other people's values?

It is important that assumptions are not made about power and its dynamics, nor about values and principles. Sometimes those that appear powerless have power in other ways. Some clients/organisations may be fully aware of the aid system and will be adept at 'working the system' to gain favour with donors. Some are quite transparent about this, others not so. A change agent might encourage more transparency; as such an understanding will better inform the motivation behind the capacity building process. It may also be part of the design of a capacity building programme that all stakeholders become more self, power and values aware.

> **Critical thoughts**
>
> Are your values and principles shared by the organisation for which you work? If there are incompatible values, what needs to be done?
>
> Is there a 'values fit' between you and the organisation for which you work? If not what are the implications and what action needs to be taken?

SUMMARY

- Any individual working with an organisation in a change process will bring with them a set of values that are shaped by their own history. Making explicit these values and principles will lead to increased self-awareness of how they may be influencing the capacity building process.
- Roles are based on the principle of who is responsible for the change process and the growth of the client or partner. Different intervention levels may be more appropriate at different times in the design and implementation of the capacity building programme.

- The change agent brings into the process preferred **styles** which reflect a deeper set of values that may or may not be consciously articulated by the individual.
- The challenge to those working on capacity building lies in building self confidence and establishing the means to clearly understand the underlying power dynamics which will shape the design, implementation and outcomes of any interventions.

RECOMMENDED READING

Harrison, R. 'Personal Power and Influence in Organizational Development' in *The Collected Papers of Roger Harrison*. McGraw-Hill, 1995.

Lippitt, G and Lippitt, R. *The Consulting Process in Action*. University Associates Inc, 1986

Chapter 7
Agendas

Introduction

This chapter looks at the 'head' of the body framework – the agendas behind any capacity building initiative. The head gives us a sense of direction, but it is located firmly on the top of the spinal column – the values and principles that provide the base for that sense-making. As has been seen in Part Two, organisational and individually held values shape the approach taken to capacity building. They are also the primary influence on the motivations for engaging in this work in the first place. Thus, they will influence the answer to the critical question of 'capacity building for what?'. This chapter explores the different ways that question may be answered. Part Three introduces the 'legs' of the framework – the design of any specific capacity building initiative. However, it is first essential to understand the underlying agenda which will influence the design choices made.

The term 'agenda' is not used in a negative sense – it refers to the underlying motivations behind an organisation's actions, decisions etc.

Agenda

Identifying agendas

Before looking more specifically at the shaping of any capacity building initiative in Part Three it is important to understand how the broad sense of direction is provided. This refers to the underlying reason or agenda why the organisation sponsoring the work is engaging in it. This agenda may or may not be specifically expressed as a broad aim for the organisation's civil society capacity building work as a whole.

It is possible to identify several areas in which choices are being made about the overall direction of the work. These are:

1. The position taken on whether strong civil society capacity is seen largely as an end in itself, or as a means to another, predefined, end.

2. The initial answer to the question – 'Capacity building for what?'

Means/end

The means/end tension refers to the need to be clear whether the initiative sees increased capacity as:

- A means to another end, e.g. reduced prevalence of HIV/AIDS or increased livelihood opportunities.

or

- An end in itself, e.g. a healthier organisation, able to survive and fulfil its mission (organisational level) or strong and confident CSOs engaging in all spheres of societal life (sector level).

An approach which stresses the **means to another end** emphasises increased capacity to perform in relation to some predefined change objectives in society at large. This approach is linked to the 'functional' notion of capacity.

⇔ Part One, Chapter 1, on understanding capacity

As indicated earlier, this approach may include a heavy emphasis on developing the absorption capacity of participating CSOs. That is, ensuring the CSOs have the capacity to effectively absorb resources provided by a donor agency, for example use project funding in a transparent, effective and efficient manner.

The majority of development agencies, including INGOs, are likely to agree that their capacity building programming emphasises the 'functional'. The work to support civil society capacity development is an instrument which can contribute towards achieving their own organisational mission and strategic objectives regarding the changes they are working for in society at large. This forms part of their agenda for capacity building.

An approach which stresses capacity development as an **end in itself** also relates to the *intrinsic* nature of capacity, that is, an emphasis on the organisation's ability/power to 'be' – to fulfil its mission.

⇔ Part One, Chapter 1, on understanding capacity

By working primarily with the notion of robust capacity which may be utilised in any arena (political, social, economic etc), this approach will emphasise the strengthening of the organisation's or sector's resilience as an end in itself. The specific objectives of the increased capacity may not necessarily be predefined.

There are a number of **influencing factors** which will determine which approach is preferred:

- The model or vision that is held of the role that civil society and its organisations play in the context of change and development.
- This is linked to the value placed on CSOs as actors for change.
- The vision that the sponsoring organisation has of itself as a change agent.
- The need of the sponsoring organisation to clearly articulate all of its programme work in a way which illustrates how it is contributing to the organisation's overall development objectives.

> **? Critical thoughts**
>
> Are you able to identify whether the underlying approach you are taking to your capacity building work is primarily 'functional' or 'intrinsic'?
>
> How far are you familiar with how your organisation's vision and values are influencing this?

Not all agencies would necessarily be overt about this, particularly if taking a more instrumentalist approach. It may well be that there is some degree of denial, or self-deception, that operates. For example, in order to invest in North–South partnership development, an INGO may well downplay any links between the stated purpose of its capacity building work and its own broader organisational strategic objectives. It may wish to stress instead its commitment to supporting the agenda of its partners without appearing to gain too much benefit for itself.

> **👁 Case example**
>
> Organisation Alpha's mission is focused on education, and it has recently defined a strategic objective around achieving improvements in young girls' access to secondary education. In country Y it has been working for the past four years, in partnership with a coalition of local NGOs, to influence the government's education policies. Alpha has provided funding for the secretariat staffing and is now contemplating providing resources for strengthening the organisational capacity of the coalition. The coalition has prioritised two areas: strengthening its internal governance and improving its communications functions. As funds are limited, Alpha has to decide how best to use these resources. In the dialogue with the partners, the Alpha representative stresses the importance of the ownership of the capacity building initiative being with the coalition. They emphasise the long-term nature of the relationship, and the commitment to support the mission of the coalition. Finally, they announce that Alpha only has funds to support to the communications improvements.
>
> The underlying agenda for Alpha is to provide capacity building support to improve access to education. When hard choices have to be made about allocating limited resources, the priority was placed on investing in the capacity area which was felt most likely to improve the advocacy performance of the coalition, and to produce results related to increasing girls' access to secondary education. However, this reasoning was not explained with the partners, and the coalition members were left without a clear idea of why one capacity area was prioritised over another.

> **? Critical thoughts**
>
> How far are you being explicit about the approach you are taking to this work in your dialogue with the participants of your capacity building initiative?
>
> Are you able to clearly articulate this in terms of the links to your organisation's strategy and mission?

Answering 'Capacity building for what?'

The answer to this question will be linked to the degree to which there is an overall approach which emphasises either a functional or intrinsic notion of capacity and capacity building. It is useful to ask this question as a way of arriving at a more explicit expression of the agenda behind the capacity building work. This may be in the form of a written aim which articulates why the sponsoring organisation is engaged in this work.

Examples of written aims shaped by functional and intrinsic approaches:

- **Functional:**
  The development of civil society capacity to contribute to the reduction of poverty and vulnerability.
  The development of civil society capacity to contribute to political and social reform.

- **Intrinsic:**
  The development of civil society capacity to organise itself by means of diverse, sustainable, healthy entities which contribute to human wellbeing, societal change and development in ways which are appropriate to their missions and objectives.

Looking more closely at the predominant functional approach, it is possible to discern the ways in which global policy trends have influenced the answers to the 'capacity building for what?' question. Examples of this include poverty reduction strategies; climate change; security concerns; reduction of the state role or privatisation of public services; globalisation of trade and markets; geo-political environments etc. Each change in policy or shift in emphasis in turn change the types of capacities that are deemed necessary for the new challenges and opportunities.

Examples of policy trends which have influenced capacity building:

- Cold war policies – prioritising civil society capacity building for containment purposes, e.g. in Latin America
- Globalisation – trade and markets – strengthening civil society capacities to compete; labour markets and civil society capacity to defend labour rights
- Reduction of state role/privatisation of public services – strengthening civil society capacity for service delivery; contracting; compacts/social partnerships
- Decentralisation – strengthening capacity of community based organisations; local CSO engagement in policy influencing

- Poverty reduction strategies and MDGs – strengthening civil society capacity to contribute by means of service delivery; policy influencing or monitoring; building cross-sector relational capacity
- Climate change – strengthening civil society capacity for natural disaster management/risk reduction
- Security concerns – strengthening civil society capacity for containment purposes and for increased accountability.

As the majority of those who engage with capacity building do take a functional approach, it is critical to be an aware of the ways in which the global policy trends have influenced the agendas and aims of such work. This awareness is even more critical if the process of setting the agenda and defining the aim is one which is 'external'; that is, initiated, designed, planned and delivered by 'some' (usually those in position of power) to 'others' who have had no say in the matter. Unfortunately, this is still often the case in capacity building programming.

Part Three, Chapters 2 and 3

> **Critical thoughts**
>
> How clear are you about the ways in which the external policy environment has influenced the setting of your agenda for capacity building?
>
> Who defines the answer to the 'capacity building for what?' question in your experience?
>
> What processes are in place to enable different voices to be heard and taken into account when establishing the answer?
>
> How do power dynamics express themselves when choosing the answer?

SUMMARY

This chapter presents the reader with different motivations for engagement in capacity building work, i.e. the underlying agendas. The agenda may or may not be specifically expressed as a broad aim for the organisation's capacity building work. Consideration about the overall direction of the work will include the following choices:

1. The position taken on seeing strong civil society capacity largely as an end in itself, or as a means to another, predefined, end.
2. The initial, 'higher order' answer to the question – 'Capacity building for what?'

RECOMMENDED READING

James, R and Hailey, J. *Capacity Building for NGOs: Making it Work*. INTRAC, 2007

Ubels, J et al. *Capacity Development: From Theory to SNV's Practice*. SNV paper, 2006

Official donor agendas:

Siri, G. *The World Bank and Civil Society Development: Exploring Two Courses of Action for Capacity Building'*. World Bank Working Paper, 2002

Whyte, A. *Landscape Analysis of Donor Trends in International Development (Human & Institutional Capacity Building – Rockefeller Foundation Series No.2)*. New York, 2004.

Supporting Capacity Development: The UNDP Approach. UNDP, 2007

Part Three
Designing and implementing a capacity building programme

Introduction

Part Three considers the programme shape, the 'grounding' of the overall capacity building framework. This part relates to the 'legs' of the body. Having strong legs will involve making a series of choices about:

Programme shape

- programme nature (Chapters 1 and 5)
- scope and target population (Chapters 2 and 3)
- levels of intervention (Chapters 3 and 5)
- goal and objectives (Chapter 3)
- timeframe (Chapter 3)
- intervention strategies and activities, and choice of appropriate methods and tools (Chapter 4)
- roles and relationships (Chapter 6)
- resourcing (Chapter 7)
- monitoring, evaluation and impact assessment (Chapter 8)

The choices that each individual organisation makes in relation to the points above will determine the ultimate shape of the programme.

One of the key challenges facing anyone designing capacity building work is how best to reflect the strategic nature of the intervention. **Chapter 1** proposes that one way to achieve this is through taking a 'programmatic approach'. It introduces three ways in which the concept of a programmatic approach may be applied to capacity building work and aims to facilitate reflection about which might be the most appropriate fit to the reader's context and organisation.

Chapter 2 leads the reader into the substance of capacity building programming. It covers the process of gathering information and analysing the context and needs that must be considered when defining the goal and objectives of the initiative. The mapping phase is the start of the 'legwork' – providing the data which will inform the design and programming choices and ground it within its context. A framework requires 'strong legs' to steady the body, and take the person in the desired direction.

The remainder of Part Three explores a range of programming choices and issues for reflection. In **Chapter 3** the levels of intervention for capacity building programming are introduced. These range from sector level, sub-sector level, organisational level and individual level capacity building. None of these are mutually exclusive and there is a challenge to ensure coherence across the different types of interventions and levels.

Another key challenge is clarity on **whose capacity** is being targeted. For example, broad sector-level capacity building initiatives must be very clear on which organisations, networks etc are considered to be within the denominated civil society sector. The term 'strategic partners' must also be clear and the values that an organisation places on partnerships will play a role in the scope of the partner capacity building work to be undertaken.

The same principles apply to setting goals and objectives as for any programme, however in Chapter 3 some additional factors to consider are introduced:

- being clear on the answer to the 'capacity for what?' question
- being aware of the possibility of unplanned opportunities arising
- ensuring that the formulation of capacity building goals and objectives truly addresses relationships of power
- implementing a design approach which seeks to ensure ownership throughout.

Chapter 4 introduces intervention strategies and activities as elements of the programme design that will form part of the implementation stage. These are the most visible and tangible elements of the programme. The chapter identifies issues to consider when choosing the best strategies to meet the programme objectives, and the range of activities available. This chapter also highlights the importance of combining the most appropriate individual activities and ensuring coherence and linkages across them. Furthermore, it emphasises that, if strategies and activities are to be successful in their implementation, then stakeholders who have an interest in or will be affected by these strategies and activities should be part of the design of them.

Returning to the issues raised in Chapter 1 about taking a programmatic approach, there are many options available for the overall packaging of the capacity building work. **Chapter 5** explores three approaches to shaping a capacity building programme, as commonly promoted by sponsors of such initiatives:

- Civil society sector/sub-sector strengthening programmes
- Partner capacity building programmes
- Programmes emphasising long-term organisation development of individual organisations.

It highlights the similarities and differences between each of the approaches and asks the reader some critical questions in relation to the most appropriate approach for their capacity building work.

Chapter 6 focuses on the role of the 'sponsoring' organisation in the provision of capacity building support. A sponsoring organisation is one which is involved in promoting a capacity building initiative. It would generally apply to INGOs. Chapter 6 covers an overview of supply and demand issues; explores the roles available to those who are sponsoring capacity building programmes, including a best practice model; and looks at the critical factors to be considered when making choices about the roles to be played.

Capacity building programme resourcing issues will affect every aspect of decision making about the overall design and implementation of the programme. The programme may have a clear goal and objectives, but if funding is not available then it will not happen. Or an organisation may be clear about its role in the programme, but does not have the expertise to take on that role. It is far more likely that resourcing is a limiting factor which may inhibit overall design and implementation and therefore is a serious consideration early on in the design phase. **Chapter 7** focuses on six areas of resourcing that should be considered: dedicated funds and funding sources, time, specialised in-house expertise, staff with competencies, a broad knowledge base and relevant relationships.

Chapter 8 explores monitoring, evaluation and impact assessment, looking at some of the challenges that surround assessment of capacity building programmes and ways to overcome these. It highlights the importance of a learning culture that becomes a 'way of life' in any capacity building programme; the need to change a mindset from one of measurable and tangible results to one of flexibility, adaptability, and uncertainty; and applying methodologies such as the concept of plausible association, baseline data and innovative participatory methods to assess the impact of programmes more effectively.

Chapter 1
A programmatic approach to capacity building

Programme shape

One of the key challenges facing anyone embarking upon the design of capacity building work is how best to reflect the strategic nature of the intervention. This chapter proposes that one way to achieve this is through taking a 'programmatic approach'. The chapter covers three ways in which this concept is applied to capacity building work, with the aim of facilitating reflection about which might be most appropriate to different contexts and needs. The chapter will also help the reader think through the issues and challenges in relation to the fit of capacity building programming with their organisation's overall programme policies, instruments and systems.

Part Three, Chapter 6

The questions posed relate to the shaping of the work, and thus the 'legs' of the body framework. However, for the reader to make choices about the most appropriate shape of the capacity building approach, they will need to draw on the conceptual references located in the 'arms'. On the issue of 'programmatic' shaping, the reader will need to be clear on how their organisation understands programmatic work and what organisational policy documents are available to guide them.

What do we mean by the 'programmatic approach'?

A programmatic approach is one which demonstrates a number of key characteristics that are commonly found in programmes. There are a number of different definitions of programmes, including:

> 'A coherent and co-ordinated set of interventions by Trocaire and partners, working together at different levels towards an overall common objective and a platform of action, in line with Trocaire's mission and strategic thematic priorities.'
> (Trocaire)

> 'A programme will have a range of strategies working towards defined outcomes. A programme can include a collection of inter-related projects and activities. It may be a mixture of development, relief, advocacy, networking and capacity building.'
> (INTRAC)

'… a group of related projects, and/or (ongoing) activities managed in a co-ordinated way and aiming at achieving a set of predetermined common (programme) objectives.'
(MDF)

The definitions vary in complexity – with the third one the most minimalist understanding. However, all three definitions understand that a programme involves working towards a **common strategic objective and addressing it in all its dimensions**. Programmes offer the opportunity to tackle challenges in more depth and enable us to frame our work at different levels and with a diversity of target groups.

Common key characteristics of a programmatic approach

- Focus on a longer-term goal and/or more complex objectives directed at 'deep change'
- Seeks coherence across multiple interventions at different levels
- Synergy between different strategies
- Long-term framework within which various cycles of shorter-term projects or interventions may take place
- High degree of coordination across activities
- Offers opportunity of working with a diversity of relationships
- Contains strong element of shared learning
- Will evolve and change over time
- Permeable boundaries i.e. projects/partners can be drawn in or phased out
- May have context-specific diversity of interventions which contribute in different ways to the overarching objectives.

The example below illustrates a number of different programmatic forms. Each organisation will decide for itself the appropriate typology and the range of expressions that it can encompass.

> **Case example: typology of UNDP programmes and projects implemented in 12 countries under their programme approach**
>
> - **focused multisectoral programmes** – programmes that concentrate efforts on a specific task, a precise geographical area or a clear set of beneficiaries.
> - **focused sectoral or subsectoral programmes** – programmes that link components or sub-projects in a coherent, coordinated fashion.
> - **umbrella programmes** – projects managed independently but placed under a single programme to achieve greater simplicity and flexibility in the allocation of funds: considered by UNDP as a valid design type as long as the projects concerned share a common purpose and a functioning coordination mechanism.
> - **programmatic projects** – projects that, to a certain degree, are strategic, well coordinated, nationally owned and participatory but managed independently; a type that UNDP considers is appropriate either in situations where the Government is not convinced of the relevance of the programme approach, or for unforeseen and strategic interventions even within the programme approach.
> - **unfocused programmes** – programmes that encompass a wide array of sectors, beneficiaries and regions and tend to be highly complex and difficult to manage: a design type that UNDP considers should be avoided.
> - **programme ersatz** – indiscriminate grouping of independent, uncoordinated, scattered projects under the title of "programme" to give the appearance of applying the programme approach.
> - **Uncoordinated/scattered projects** – projects that are designed and implemented without any linkages among them.
>
> (Source: UNDP Evaluation Unit, www.undp.org)

> **Critical thought**
>
> Are you clear about the programming approach you are taking in your capacity building work?

Different programmatic approaches

It is critical that there is coherence between the choices made when considering options for capacity building work and the overall organisational understanding of programmatic working. In addition to ensuring a good fit with your organisation's general approach to programmes, you may wish to consider the following three common approaches to capacity building programmes:

a. 'Stand-alone' programmes

This is dedicated capacity building work which is considered as a programme in its own right.

> Examples include:
>
> - A **civil society strengthening** programme in a particular country, region or as a global initiative, encompassing many of the characteristics above in a systematic and complex manner. One definition of such a focused civil society programme is '… a cohesive programme with interventions at different levels contributing to an explicit primary purpose of strengthening civil society as a sector.' (Trocaire)
> - **Focused sector** work dedicated to strengthening a particular type of organised civil society, for example community organisations, social movements, advocacy networks, etc.
> - A **partner capacity building** programme which may be geographic or sectoral. This would tend to focus on a target group of organisations with whom there is an ongoing relationship.
> - **Specific capacity building interventions** or **methods** expressed programmatically, such as a civil society leadership development programme or an international exchange programme.

b. Cross-cutting programmes

These are capacity building activities incorporated within broader sectoral, thematic or geographic programmes. This may be a rather minimalist approach towards capacity building and it often does not provide an opportunity to think and act strategically. So, in cases where you do not have stand-alone capacity building programmes it is necessary to consider how to ensure a strategic approach.

It may help to think through, using the following questions, how to design this cross-cutting capacity element to reflect some or all of the key characteristics of a programmatic approach:

- What is the overall capacity building objective to which all of the cross-cutting initiatives might contribute?
- How will you ensure that the activities and approaches reinforce each other, rather than become a fragmented and disparate group of activities?
- How will you build in learning about the progress of this cross-cutting element?
- What are the resourcing implications of working this way? For example, who will ensure consistency and coherence in how the capacity building element is managed?
- Are you clear on what you will be measuring with regard to the possible outcomes and longer-term impact of this work?

> **Case example**
>
> Organisation Y operates with three sector programmes in the 15 countries in which it is working: livelihoods; HIV/AIDS and education. Each country office is responsible for developing its programme work in line with overall organisational objectives identified for these three sectors. In addition, each country team has to identify partner capacity building initiatives to be undertaken. The field staff discuss capacity building needs with partners as part of the overall process of developing the partnership project for the three programmes. The capacity building activities are then incorporated within the individual partnership agreements defined with each CSO partner working in the three sectors.
>
> The organisation has created a headquarters position of Capacity Building Adviser, and has developed a series of guidelines and reference materials for field staff. The adviser's role is to ensure the guidelines are put into practice, and also to review project evaluations in order to identify successes, challenges and lessons learnt in the capacity building work.

c. 'Mainstreamed' capacity building

Mainstreaming involves both answering the questions set out above in relation to a cross-cutting approach, but also going further and seeking to achieve critical shifts in attitude and behaviour. Mainstreaming is a strategy for making capacity development an integral dimension of the design, implementation, monitoring and evaluation of policies and programmes. Capacity building becomes something which is core to *the way* your organisation works as well as to *what* it does.

> **Case example: civil society strengthening in all programmes**
>
> The objective of this component is to ensure that all of Trocaire's work contributes, in some way, to the further strengthening of civil society ... This means that programmes with no clear civil society strengthening dimension would be an exception, and that a strong rationale would be required for any such work.
>
> (Source: Trocaire's Civil Society Policy, July 2006)

Examples of mainstreamed capacity building include:

- Starting every initiative with the question, 'how will the way we approach this work contribute to strengthening the civil society actors involved, or promote or protect the space for civic action?'.
- Defining capacity building outputs for every initiative taken.
- Ensuring that every evaluation, review and other learning processes incorporates questions for reflection on how civil society capacity has been affected.
- Reflecting on how your organisation's capacity may be affected by the work and relationships it is engaged with.

One benefit of mainstreaming capacity building is the fact that there is greater potential for your own organisation to learn and develop as a result of the attitude and behaviour changes that are implicit within such an approach. Another benefit is that there is a clearer agenda on capacity building, with greater potential for developing an approach to strengthening civil society actors in a way which moves beyond the purely functional or potentially instrumental approaches.

> **Critical thoughts**
>
> The decision to mainstream capacity building should be based on a clear analysis of why your organisation decides to mainstream certain issues. Do you have this analysis?
>
> What does this mean in terms of internal changes within the organisation?

Benefits of the programmatic approach to capacity building

These may include:

- enables **strategic thinking** about processes of change – arguably a fundamental precondition for effective development work
- potential for **increased impact** in terms of sustainable changes, when working programmatically as opposed to working with isolated or fragmented capacity building initiatives
- the planning process helps to **clarify the purpose** and **contribution** of each specific intervention in relation to a strategic goal
- facilitates **linkages** between initiatives
- helps identify opportunities for **alliances** and **collaboration** with others
- provides a useful framework for **learning**
- enables an organisation to bring to play a number of its **diverse competencies**
- can encourage **flexibility**, lateral thinking and create opportunities for 'emergent' work.

SUMMARY

This chapter proposes a programmatic approach to capacity building, and highlights three ways in which this can be applied:

Stand-alone capacity building programmes where dedicated capacity building work is a programme in its own right, rather than being a dimension of a broader programme.

Cross-cutting element of capacity building where capacity building activities are incorporated within broader sectoral, thematic or geographic programmes.

Mainstreamed capacity building is more than a cross-cutting element as capacity building is a critical lens which influences the design of policies, programmes, systems, behaviours etc. Therefore it becomes core to *the way* an organisation works as well as to *what* it does.

RECOMMENDED READING

Lusthaus, C, Adrien, M-H and Morgan, P. *Integrating Capacity Development into Project Design and Evaluation. Approach and Frameworks (Monitoring and Evaluation Paper 5).* 2000

Chapter 2
Mapping and analysis

Introduction

This chapter leads into the substance of capacity building programming – the 'legs' of the framework. It refers to the process of gathering information and analysing the context, and the needs that must be considered in order to define the focus for the capacity building programme. Reference to the more specific work of assessing the capacities of individual organisations can be found in Part Three, Chapter 6.

Programme shape

Mapping and analysis, when thoroughly undertaken, provide a firm foundation for the programme. Other terms are also used to describe activities carried out during this phase, such as 'scoping' and 'needs assessment'. This chapter gives an overview on what is involved in mapping work and suggests a variety of methods and tools. Two case studies are provided as illustrations: the first describing a broad civil society sector mapping, the second a more focused exercise.

The purpose of mapping or scoping exercises

Being clear about the purpose of mapping and scoping exercises will help decide what information needs to be gathered and how to do it. There may be different types of exercises reflecting different purposes, for example:

- Exercises to help understand the broad civil society sector in a particular region or country, in order to identify an appropriate focus for future capacity building work.

> **Case example:**
> Organisation Beta wants to strengthen CSOs because they believe that civil society actors are critical to the future development of a country. However, they will need information on the specific characteristics of the sector in a particular country context, in order to help them identify how they may best support this strengthening. In this case, an initial broad sweep mapping of the sector may help define the scope of the programme.

- Where a particular focus has already been established, the exercise may concentrate on identifying capacity issues facing the range of actors which fall within that focus.

> **Case example:**
>
> INGO X wishes to strengthen CSOs working in HIV/AIDS, but is not clear what the more specific answer to the 'capacity for what?' question would be within that sub-sector. Is it around increased capacity to deliver HIV/AIDS prevention/awareness programmes? Is it increased capacity of local CSOs to ensure that government policies take into account a particular, marginalised group? Is it about local research capacity to ensure that HIV/AIDS programmes are adequately informed? Should it be focused on networks and coalitions, on individual NGOs or grassroots groups or a mix of all of these? The mapping exercise here would include a strong capacity assessment component, and would also have a pre-determined set of informants i.e. those who are engaged in HIV/AIDS and the health sector.

- To 'scope' the potential approach to capacity building with an identified set of actors, for example for a partner capacity building programme.

> **Case example:**
>
> INGO Z wishes to establish a long-term programme of support to its local CSO partners, over and beyond the current funding support which it provides to the partners' programmes of work. It is not sure how best to approach this and wishes to explore various options with the partners. The exercise would therefore use participative methodologies in order to generate interest and commitment of the partners and to ensure a demand-led programme.

Having established the purpose of the mapping, it is important to communicate this clearly to the participants and not to raise unrealistic expectations about the benefits and scope a future programme might have.

Data selection

The next step is to focus the exercise to ensure the right information is gathered. As well as specific information determined by the purpose, other useful data includes:

- **The enabling and constraining environment** i.e. factors which facilitate or obstruct effective CSO action, such as the legislation which covers CSO activity; the fiscal regime; media attitudes towards and coverage of the sector; ease of access to information; the degree of public support to the sector; the strength of the volunteering ethos; the general political climate etc.

    Part Three, Chapter 3

- **Relationships and power dynamics** (for example within and between different sectors). What legitimacy and reputation does the civil society sector have and how does it relate to other sectors? What level of engagement with government does it have and what are the current issues being negotiated? What informal and formal power dynamics are present, and how does this affect the sector and its potential for growth? What are the contextual dynamics as regards gender relations and CSOs?

- **Civil society actors** (for example, number of organisations and network groupings, their purpose and funding).What types of CSOs exist, how long have they been established and for what purpose? How secure is the sector's funding base and what are the sources? How does this affect and impact on civil society development? How strong are networks and how do they relate to each other?

⇔ Part Three, Chapter 3

- **Analysis of the current capacity building provision**, (the 'supply' side as well as the 'demand' side). As a capacity building provider it will be important to know who the other actors are – will there be duplication and what lessons can be learnt? Are there civil society support organisations on the ground that can help in the programme development and implementation? If there is little understanding of capacity building, how can awareness be raised and other actors encouraged into the field?

⇔ Part Three, Chapter 7

- **Assessing existing capacities as well as capacity needs** – by acknowledging what is already present and making use of it. For example, local knowledge of the political situation, or strong networks and linkages, or by making a thorough participatory capacity assessment with key stakeholders to help identify the most important capacity strengths and gaps.

Methods and tools for mapping

Having established the purpose of the mapping and which data would be most useful, the next step is to decide on the most appropriate methods and tools. Mapping involves selecting and gathering data. It also provides an opportunity, perhaps for the first time, to begin the process of building relationships, identifying key actors and hidden voices, and getting a feel for the situation, all of which will be essential for the future success of a capacity building programme. Most importantly, the mapping should involve major stakeholders. A participatory mapping process enables capacity development from the start.

⇔ Part Two, Chapters 1, 3 and 5

Data gathering methods

There are a variety of methods for gathering data, including: focus group discussions, individual interviews, formal surveys, formal and informal workshops, participatory techniques, observation, participant observation, secondary information, technical surveys, and financial audits.

Process methods

The quality of the data gathered is affected by the process and methods used, as well as the approach, attitude and behaviour of the practitioner. Whilst using participatory methods requires skilful facilitation and additional time, one tangible and immediate benefit is that stakeholders are more involved in deciding the areas for investigation and analysis. Thus they are part of the design of the process and the generation and diagnosis of data. Stakeholders begin to feel positive about the planned programme, having been involved in opinion sharing at this early stage. The groundwork done in mapping and analysis may reap dividends for the future success of the programme.

Part Two, Chapters 3 and 5

Examples of the benefits of using participatory process methods include:

- Establishing roles and ownership
- Building capacity in the mapping phase
- Bringing together a range of stakeholders
- Sharing ideas about capacity building

- **Establishing roles and ownership**

Using participatory process methods will help establish ownership of both the mapping exercise and the future programme early on. It is important to try and avoid the 'expert' research/consultancy tone and engage representatives from different stakeholder groups using facilitative methods. Avoid using stakeholders for 'extracting' information but engage them, for example by involving them in **planning the mapping and analysis exercises**, **continuous dialogue** through **periodic review meetings** or **forming an advisory group** for the planning and design phase of the programme.

> **Critical thought**
>
> Working with stakeholders from the beginning to identify the key questions (rather using pre-set ones) will provide a firm basis for establishing ownership.

- **Building capacity in the mapping phase**

Process methods also provide an opportunity to begin capacity building even at the early mapping and analysis stage. For example, inviting different target groups to an early **process workshop** provides an opportunity to analyse the environment and the challenges it presents to the civil society sector. This allows common organisational capacity challenges to be identified, which can form the basis of a future capacity building programme. This avoids the typical feedback workshop where the results of the investigation are discussed for the first time at the end of the exercise. In addition, introducing a workshop early on can set the tone of the overall approach – one which emphasises the importance of building relationships across civil society actors.

> **? Critical thoughts**
>
> How explicit is your plan to build capacity through the process of designing the capacity building programme?
>
> What implications does such an approach have for you and your organisation's skills, time, resources?

- **Bringing together a range of stakeholders**

Process methods can also ensure that stakeholders from different and sometimes opposing sectors and viewpoints come together to discuss issues that affect them. For example, in countries working to a democratisation agenda, where the civil society sector may have previously worked in opposition to government, early dialogue at **participatory mapping workshops** can help open up channels for further communication. The role of the facilitators in such workshops is critical.

⇔ Part Three, Chapter 2

> **? Critical thoughts**
>
> Bringing together stakeholders with strongly held and opposing views is challenging. As well as considering the motives and power dynamics of participants, be clear about your own power, biases and blind spots in relation to the context and stakeholders.

- **Sharing ideas about capacity building**

Finally, process methods can help clarify understanding of capacity building between all parties, for example, client group, practitioner, consultant, support organisation, or donor. Such concepts do not always travel well. The introduction of the concepts and examples of good practice into process workshops early on will not only provide an opportunity to learn about levels of awareness of capacity building itself, but help shape the future design and implementation of the programme.

> **? Critical thoughts**
>
> Are you making assumptions about stakeholders' understanding of capacity building?
>
> Have you created opportunities for discussion to clarify and share such concepts?

The following case studies provide examples of an approach using process methods. Those carrying out the mapping (consultants for a civil society support organisation) worked with local partners, and incorporated a developmental process approach from the beginning.

The case example below shows a broader mapping exercise, using process methods to help understand the context, actors and civil society sector, prior to designing the capacity building programme.

> ### Case example: EU Support to Civil Society Programme in Uganda
>
> The programme aimed to increase the role of civil society in the development process by building the capacity of CSOs to perform an advocacy role vis-à-vis government and be effective service deliverers.
>
> **The process**
>
> Two international civil society support organisations together with a Ugandan counterpart carried out a two-phase study: mapping and feasibility. Stakeholders were involved from the beginning to create ownership of the results. This was done by:
>
> 1) The consultancy team facilitated a 'process consultation' with a variety of stakeholders, including the Ugandan government.
>
> 2) This approach allowed for maximum participation of CSOs through organisational self-analysis and strategy design.
>
> Stakeholders were involved directly in:
>
> - **Inception meeting** where objectives were presented and roles and methodology of the study were shared.
> - **Mapping study** that analysed networks, and the capacities and effectiveness of CSOs.
> - **Feedback workshop** where comments were received on the consultancy team's initial proposals. Small groups were established to participate in the feasibility study.
> - **Feasibility study** where further analysis of specific issues was carried out together and preparation of the proposal took place.
> - **Final feedback workshop** whereby a broader representation of CSOs could comment on the proposal.
>
> For the first three steps a variety of participatory methods (for example workshops and focus group discussions) were used to analyse the context, stakeholders and their capacities, vulnerabilities and relationships.
>
> The following questions formed the basis of the discussions:
>
> - What are the aims of the organisation (and are they the same at different levels)?
> - What are the aims of the organisation (and are they the same at different levels)?
> - How do CSOs organise themselves to achieve these aims?
> - What is un/successful and why and what factors determine this?
> - What has been learnt from these experiences and how would you organise differently in the future?

> The feedback workshops provided opportunities for discussion about progress. In addition, the consultants suggested that direct contact with key stakeholders following the workshop could provide an opportunity to express opinions which could not be aired during the workshops.
>
> **Key learnings**
>
> The study was successful in its focus on CSO effectiveness and impact determined by four dimensions seen as influencing effective CSO actions: the operational space; resources, values and impact. The study looked at the space (environment, legal, political, attitude of government to CSO activity, legitimacy of CSOs in the public view etc) in which CSOs were operating. It also considered the type, availability and sustainability of resources accessible to CSOs. The impact and capacity of CSOs was considered and differentiated by type of CSO as well as the focus of activities, especially the welfare versus policy engagement and rural versus urban. In relation to impact and values, CSOs were facilitated to analyse the factors which influenced their successes and failures and learning that they took from this. In this case the data collection activities involved the stakeholders in self assessment which had an intrinsic value beyond the needs of the programme design team.

The case study below is a more focused exercise where the aim of the capacity building programme is specific, some partners are already established and previous learning from other geographical areas can be applied. Again, process methods are used to ensure a capacity building element early on. The case highlights the importance of being pragmatic in difficult circumstances, and identifying appropriate partners. This relies on existing local knowledge, previous experience, and relationship building.

> **Case example: Save the Children Iraq Capacity Building Programme, 2003–04**
>
> The programme aimed to build the capacities of local NGOs to effectively respond to child rights challenges in three prioritised sectors (food security, child protection and education). The organisation had worked for many years with northern Iraqi partners, developing skills in areas such as rights based assessment and programming. This experience had been positive, albeit ad hoc. It was now felt appropriate to work in a different way with the remaining partners due to the changed external context. There were new internal organisational development issues and changes to their role and relationships with others (local government, central authorities, donors, INGOs).
>
> There was also an opportunity to extend this work into three new geographic areas and invest in a more systematic approach by raising resources for a specific capacity building programme. It was hoped to use the platform of the northern experience to link in with similar initiatives being discussed by other NGOs (local and international) via a coordinating committee. Finally, there was a desire to explore creative approaches to capacity building as alternatives to the rather more 'instrumental' programmes expected to be introduced under the auspices of the official agencies.

INTRAC worked with the Save the Children Iraq programme team on an initial scoping exercise, which entailed:

- **Initial methodological and conceptual workshop.** This aimed to:
  - establish the parameters for the scoping exercise
  - establish shared understanding on capacity building concepts and frameworks
  - review methods and tools for use during the exercise (INTRAC provided a range of materials which were then adapted by SC Iraq staff)
  - identify ways for at-a-distance support to be provided by INTRAC.

A total of four different mapping tools were designed.

- **In-country scoping exercise** (conducted by SC Iraq staff with at-a-distance support from INTRAC). As well as taking a first look at the capacity building needs of local organisations, the scoping exercise also undertook an initial mapping of support provision within the country and the region as well as gathering information on similar initiatives underway or being planned. As part of this exercise, capacity issues were discussed at an in-country workshop which brought together 25 local organisations for the first time across the previous Kurdistan/Iraq divide.

The outputs from this scoping exercise were used in a two-day **diagnosis and programme framing workshop**. Once the programme parameters were established, these were used by staff to write a programme proposal.

Two key lessons emerged from this experience:

1. The value added of the first methodological workshop cannot be underestimated. It took time and resources to ensure the team had clear and shared understanding of capacity building concepts and methods (the 'arms') before embarking on the scoping exercise. But this enabled there to be a common language between the INGO staff and the external consultants which facilitated the at-a-distance support during the exercise. Equally valuable was taking the time to jointly identify and adapt data gathering tools that were appropriate to the context and programme aim.

2. The in-country workshop, in itself, contributed to the capacity building aims by providing a forum for initial relationship and trust building amongst actors who had no previous engagement with each other.

Triangulation of methods and tools

As well as choosing appropriate methods and tools to enable open dialogue and stakeholder participation early on, ensuring methodological rigour is also important. Triangulation is a very useful technique for improving the quality of information and verifying data. Do not rely on one method or tool or the opinions of the most obvious stakeholders. Triangulation involves cross checking in three ways: using multiple methods and tools; using different sources of information and viewpoints; and using different people to collect the data. This technique will ensure inconsistencies in data can be more readily accounted for and will highlight areas that need further investigation.

Part Three, Chapter 8

Analysis

The mapping exercise involves analysis of the data gathered. This means reviewing and summarising the data, cross checking and verifying information with a number of stakeholders, identifying gaps where further work is needed and finally making an analysis. If there is clarity of purpose and scope of the exercise at the beginning then this will make the analysis easier.

The data gathering methods and tools chosen will also indicate the qualitative and quantitative nature of the analysis. For example, if the purpose of the mapping is to assess the capacity of a civil society sector as a whole, then data will be a combination of statistics, (e.g. numbers of CSOs and types, how many are registered or operational) and more qualitative information, such as attitudes to civil society sector, relationships with government and each other etc.

Pulling together the analysis and sharing it will be the most important step of the mapping exercise. Continuing the use of process methods in the analysis will ensure findings can be discussed and verified periodically. For example, if an advisory group has been set up from the beginning, with representatives from different stakeholder groups, assumptions and interpretations made by the data gathering team can be checked before the study ends. Advisory groups can also make judgements on the most important elements for analysis.

In all cases, the analysis must be fed back to stakeholders and participating groups. Most often this is done by a report to the commissioning agency. Sometimes, feedback workshops conclude the mapping exercise, where results are fed back and there is an opportunity for participants of the exercise to clarify or make additional comments. If a capacity building element is to be integrated into the process early on, then how the analysis is shared can be critical. The way in which the whole process is carried out will affect the sense of ownership of a capacity building programme.

Ownership by those most affected by the programme, in most cases the recipients, must be achieved, whilst maintaining buy-in from other major actors. For example, a capacity building programme focused on strengthening CSOs involved in HIV/AIDS programmes will want to ensure ownership by those organisations and their beneficiaries, whilst at the same time commitment and support by the government health department, major donors and other health sector CSOs. Such an outcome will be desirable, if not essential for the future programme. However, it is important to be aware of potential conflicts of interests, at the same time of being continuously mindful of the original purpose of the programme.

Early on, through the process of gathering and analysing your data you can start making your baseline (impact) indicators for your capacity building programme, together with your partners and/or key stakeholders.

Part Three, Chapter 8

SUMMARY

When starting to design a capacity building programme, the mapping (or scoping) and initial analysis stage is critical. These points should be remembered:

- Establish the purpose of your exercise – this will inform the choices about the process and methods used in the mapping.
- Be clear about the values and principles that underpin the capacity building programme and ensure these are clearly established in the way the mapping and analysis is carried out. If a third party is carrying out this phase ensure they are aware of and share these values and principles.
- Use process methodology to ensure ownership from the beginning and to provide a firm foundation on which the capacity building programme will be designed and implemented.

RECOMMENDED READING

Bakewell, O. *Sharpening the Development Process: A Practical Guide to Monitoring and Evaluation*. INTRAC, 2003. Ch 6, 'Data Gathering Methods'

Kaplan, A. 'Engaging with civil society in Bosnia and Herzegovina: A narrative account'. Available at www.proteusinitiative.org

This is an excellent example of an alternative account to mapping civil society as a contribution to programme design.

Chapter 3
Scope and objectives

The fundamental steps of clarifying the agenda and overall purpose behind why any organisation engages in capacity building work were highlighted in Part Two, and form the 'head' of the framework by providing a clear sense of direction. The mapping phase described in the previous chapter is the start of the 'legwork' – providing the data which will inform the design and programming choices and ground it in the context. The human frame requires strong legs to steady the body, and take the person in the desired direction. The remainder of Part Three explores how to strengthen those legs and introduces a range of programming choices and accompanying issues for reflection.

Programme shape

⊕ Framework Guide in Appendix 1. This is designed to enable the reader to systematically analyse the responses to a series of prompt questions, related to the overall programming framework presented in this book.

This chapter focuses on several of the key elements that form the legs – the choices to be made about:

- Levels of intervention
- Goal and objectives
- Scope of initiative
- Participating CSOs

Levels of intervention

⊕ Part One, Chapter 1

There are different levels of civil society association, and civil society capacity building can occur at any or all of these levels. This can be represented graphically, as in the model below. It is important to define clearly what is encompassed within each level. For INTRAC, the following applies:

Sector level capacity building: often referred to as **institutional development** or **civil society capacity building**. Working with diverse associational forms, capacity building programming at this level emphasises the capacities of the sector as a whole rather than those of any one organisation or subset of organisations. Work at this level must be based on an understanding of the history of the sector; its composition and diversity; its profile in the eyes of the general public and other sectors; its relationships both within its own society and internationally; the external challenges it faces etc. This work will address commonly shared capacity challenges and will often aim to reinforce the good practices of individual actors by disseminating them across the sector. Capacity building may encompass objectives that are focused on promoting the sector as a whole and on ensuring that the external environment enables civic association. It is likely to have strong elements of cross-sectoral work, with a major emphasis on the development of relational capacities of CSOs and actors from other sectors. In addition, this level of work will often encompass objectives which focus on building the credibility of the sector at large – often via reinforcing capacities for collective and individual accountability and transparency.

⇄ Part Three, Chapter 6

Sub-sector level is generally understood to be similar to the sector level work, except that it is focused on a particular subgroup of organisations, and thus there is more common ground amongst the actors. This subgroup may be defined geographically; on the basis of identity; or, most commonly, thematically. Here the capacity building objectives will focus on strengthening capacities in relation to specific areas of common interest (defined according to the make-up of the subgroup). Often, a strong emphasis is placed on the development of relational capacities, with a view to strengthening the collective voice and profile of that particular subset of civic actors.

⇄ Part Three, Chapter 6

Organisational capacity building deals with one organisational entity, or a 'family' of organisations with shared values, vision and mission (for example Save The Children Alliance). The type of organisation may vary in degree of formality (for example formally registered) and level of engagement in society (for example community based or an international CSO). The starting point for INTRAC is that these entities are complex open systems with capacities spanning three principal dimensions, as described in Part One. Objectives at this level may address a specific set of capacities, or may approach the development of the entity in a more holistic manner. As in the previous levels, an understanding of the context, history, composition, culture, etc of the entity is critical for effective work.

There are a number of different ways of applying this model and it is quite common that capacity building with communities and community groups appear as separate from organisational capacity building.

⇄ Part Two, Chapter 2 and Part Three, Chapter 6

Individual capacity building recognises that change happens as a result of individual as well as collective action. Similarly, changes at the personal level are key to organisational and societal development. Thus, many capacity building objectives are also framed around such things as building awareness; strengthening capacities for leadership; interpersonal communication; negotiation skills etc.

Levels of intervention

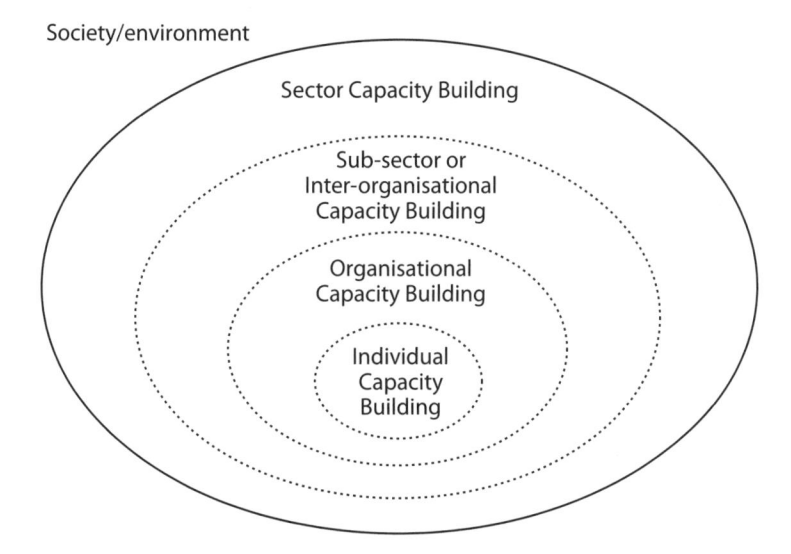

[Diagram: concentric ellipses labeled, from outermost to innermost: Society/environment, Sector Capacity Building, Sub-sector or Inter-organisational Capacity Building, Organisational Capacity Building, Individual Capacity Building]

A critical choice is that of which level or levels should be the focus of efforts to strengthen capacity. There is no one approach about which level to concentrate on – they are all important depending on your capacity building objectives, and a change in one has an impact up or down the levels.

Making linkages

It is challenging to ensure coherence and linkages between the different types of interventions and levels. The visual image below (the 'Saturn model') expresses this:

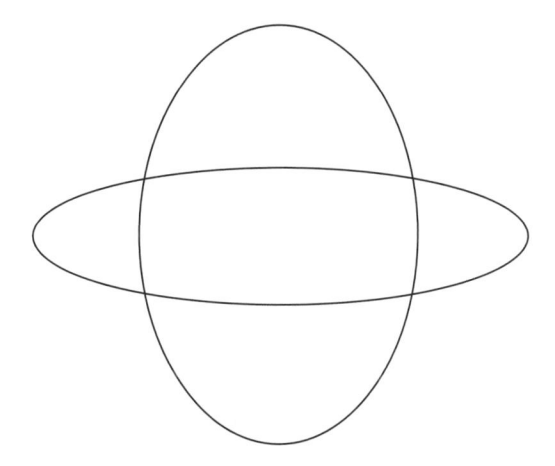

[Diagram: Saturn model — a vertical ellipse intersected by a horizontal ellipse]

Connections need to be made **between each level** (shown by the vertically oriented circle) – linking capacity building work across sectors, from sector-wide work, work with specific networks, through individual organisations to grassroots CBOs and individuals.

Some examples of ways to do this are:

- When engaged in a capacity building intervention at the level of an individual organisation, it may be appropriate to involve representatives of a relevant sector network or from another sector (private sector, local government) in particular activities, for example at a panel discussion with staff of that organisation. (Linking cross-sector level work with individual organisational capacity building)
- If involved in civic education or rights awareness raising at the level of the individual community member, build in exposure visits to CSOs working on the issue. (Linking individual level work with organisational level capacity building)
- Make sure that the content of training taking place with individual organisations contains sufficient reference to sector-wide issues. For example, advocacy training that draws on concrete case studies from initiatives undertaken by networks in the country. This could include exposure visits to discuss the specific issues of undertaking advocacy within a coalition. (Linking individual organisational level work with sub-sector capacity building)
- If working on strengthening grassroots CBOs, consider whether the work builds relationships between CBOs and intermediate NGOs or support organisations working locally.

There is also a need to make connections across groups **within the same level** (shown by the horizontally oriented circle), for example capacity building work with specific networks linked to work with similar networks elsewhere.

Some examples of ways to do this are:

- When working within a geographically focused programme, consider how to make linkages between your target organisations and similar organisations in other areas.
- How far is your analysis and mapping considering the effect that your programme may have on CSOs in a neighbouring geographic area (in the case of geographically prioritised programmes), or in a different sector (in the case of thematically focused programmes)?
- Consider the possibility of supporting the development of horizontal federations of grassroots CBOs.

Goal and objectives

The general principles of good programming apply equally to capacity building, sectoral or thematic development work. Without presuming any particular programme planning methodology is in operation, it can be assumed that the following principles should be considered when formulating the overall goal and any specific objectives for your capacity building work.

Part Two, Chapter 1

Key principles for good programming practice

- The goal and objectives should be a **relevant and appropriate response to the diagnosis** from the mapping phase.
- Programming decisions and shape are influenced by a **process of consultation**.
- The programmatic nature is **coherent** across all its elements.
- There is clarity on the **programme focus**.
- There is flexibility and **openness to unplanned opportunities that arise**.

Applying the key principles to capacity building

There are specific **factors to consider** when applying these principles to the development of capacity building goals and objectives. These reflect some of the particular challenges of this work:

- **Be clear on the answer to the 'capacity for what?' question** – the programme goal and objectives should reflect this. Clear objectives should illustrate the prioritised capacity areas, and how increased capacity will contribute to the overall changes.

> **Case example**
>
> Organisation B works on HIV/AIDS issues in 14 countries. It takes a functional approach to capacity building, with an agenda to strengthen civil society efforts to reduce HIV/AIDS incidence. Having decided to develop a capacity building programme with its Africa region partners, it carried out a scoping exercise to identify the key capacity strengths and challenges. The analysis identified increased opportunities to engage with local governments in HIV/AIDS awareness and prevention programmes.
>
> However, it also identified that most partners had little or no experience of working with local government, as they had previously focused on national advocacy work. Jointly the partners and Organisation B identified that 'capacity for what?' would be 'capacity for local government partnerships'. This provided the main programme goal: increased capacity to influence, and collaborate with, local government in HIV/AIDS awareness and prevention initiatives. The objectives addressed specific capacity areas, including: managing relationships strategically; developing an understanding of local government policies and programmes; adapting advocacy and campaigning expertise to local government context etc.

- **Responding to changing opportunities** – critical when dealing with shaping an initiative which has processes of human change at its very core. A key factor to consider is how goals and objectives can be broad enough to encompass what may emerge during implementation, whilst being focused enough to provide a reference point for assessing progress against desired results.

> **◉ Case example: continuing the example above**
>
> As the capacity building programme was being implemented, activities with local government drew the attention of other actors in the districts. The team discussed this with the partners, and agreed to run workshops on CSO–local government collaboration in the context of HIV/AIDS work. This provided an opportunity for the partners and local government officials to share their experiences with others. As the workshops progressed, some FBOs and CBOs showed an interest in engaging in the initiatives being implemented. District-level CSO coalitions were formed, which entered into collaborative initiatives with the authorities. A new capacity building objective was included; supporting the development of effective coalitions for local partnerships.

- **Ensuring that the formulation of capacity building goals and objectives truly addresses relationships of power** – does the understanding of capacity encompass 'power to' do something as well as 'ability to'.

↔ Part One, Chapters 1 and 4

- **Implementing a design which consistently seeks to ensure ownership throughout** – the critical importance of objectives for change being 'formed from within'. This is done by using participative planning processes when identifying change indicators, strategies and activities. Good practice would also include key actors in dialogue about the agendas at the heart of the initiative, and seek to identify the principal drivers of change before formulating objectives.

Scope of intervention

Formulating the goals and objectives of the capacity building work will involve a consideration of parameters, beyond those related to the different levels of operation. This means defining the scope of the initiative in terms of context, geography or theme.

↔ Part Three, Chapter 1

As indicated in the first chapter of Part Three, there are decisions to be made about the of the programmatic approach being taken – which in turn will require choices about whether to implement the capacity building work as an element of another (**thematic or sector**) programme. This is one way in which scope is clearly delineated.

> **◉ Case example**
>
> Organisation X decided to formulate its capacity building objectives within its existing sectoral programmes. Staff identified key stakeholders from each sector with whom they could collaborate in the scoping and design process. In its health sector work, the organisation had prioritised access to water and sanitation in marginalised communities. By identifying specific capacity challenges related to work for rights of access to water and sanitation, focused capacity building objectives could be formulated.

Organisations developing stand-alone dedicated capacity building programmes can use other methods to help provide focus.

Context provides focus by prioritising capacity building within contexts of, for example, post-conflict societies; societies where the civil society sector is newly (re)emerging; societies with high HIV/AIDS prevalence; contexts of rapid economic and social changes and so on.

> **◉ Case example**
>
> Organisation Y wanted to implement stand-alone civil society sector capacity building programmes. The organisation's mission incorporated work on conflict prevention and peace building. Thus it decided to limit the scope of the capacity building programmes to post-conflict countries, to provide focus and increased learning potential.

Geography is a common delineator – most organisations have priority geographic areas. A critical decision is the scale of the operation. The formulation of realistic objectives for capacity change is a very different challenge when pitched at a complex range of countries than when it is confined to a less diverse context within one society or region in a country.

All of these parameters will be influenced by the organisation's mission and strategy.

Which CSOs will participate?

A key challenge of goals and objectives is to be clear about *whose capacity* is being targeted.

For example, broad sector-level capacity building initiatives must be very clear about which organisations, associations, networks etc are considered to be within the defined civil society sector. Some 'grey area' associational forms (for example business women's associations) may be deemed by some agencies as being within the sector and by others as not.

In partner capacity building programmes, the critical issue is whether the programme is to work with all the partners of the sponsoring organisation or if further criteria for inclusion need to be established. Some organisations opt for programmes exclusively aimed at 'strategic partners' – a term which will then need further definition. The values that the organisation places on partnerships will also play a role in the definition of the scope of the partner capacity building work to be undertaken.

➲ Part Two, Chapter 6

> **? Critical thoughts**
>
> Are you clear on who is 'in' and 'outside' the civil society sector in the area of operation, as defined by your organisation and by others?
>
> To what extent do your own, and your organisation's, values play a role in defining the answer to this question?

🗝 SUMMARY

This chapter has focused on the choices to be made about levels of intervention; goal and objectives; scope of initiative and the participating CSOs.

The levels of intervention for capacity building programming are not mutually exclusive and there is a challenge to ensure coherence and links across the different types of interventions and levels.

The same principles apply to setting goals and objectives as for any programme, but with capacity building programming additional factors should be considered:

- Being clear on the answer to the 'capacity for what?' question
- Being aware of changing opportunities
- Ensuring that formulation of capacity building goals and objectives addresses relationships of power
- Use a design approach which consistently seeks to ensure ownership.

Scope of intervention requires delineating the scope of the initiative in terms of context, geography, and theme.

A key challenge is clarity on whose capacity is being targeted.

Chapter 4
Intervention strategies and activities

This chapter identifies issues to consider when choosing the appropriate strategies to meet the programme objectives, and the corresponding range of activities. Factors which affect these decisions are: the levels of intervention; the working context; culture; timeframe; resources and commitment. This chapter also highlights the importance of combining appropriate activities and ensuring coherence and links.

Programme shape

Choosing strategies

A strategy provides the overview of how to achieve the desired change. There may be a number of strategies within a capacity building programme, each made up of various activities.

> **Examples of capacity building strategies include:**
>
> - Funding, for example provision of grants for capacity building
> - Skills development
> - Infrastructure development
> - Relationship building
> - Strengthening organisational resilience
> - Investment in learning and knowledge development
> - Support the development of an 'enabling environment' for civil society.

When choosing strategies for the programme it is important to consider the effect of one strategy upon another, and to choose a range of strategies that complement each other.

For example, a programme could use funding as one element, involving individual rounds of capacity building project proposals to be presented by CSOs, appraised by a panel of experts, and approved for disbursement. What kind of relationship will this strategy have with other strategies being implemented, such as, for example, providing long-term support to the strengthening of sectoral networks? Would a competitive dynamic emerge from the funding strategy which may run counter to the collaborative dynamic being encouraged by the network strengthening strategy?

Capacity building activities

The term 'capacity building activities' is used here to refer to the range of concrete actions to be taken within the chosen strategies. They are the specific steps towards the achievement of the desired capacity changes. Sometimes other terms are used interchangably, such as 'capacity building methods' or 'capacity building interventions'.

Examples of commonly used capacity building activities:

- Training – most frequently used but possibly most superficial in impact
- Technical assistance – particularly frequent in official agency programmes
- Management consultancies, for example on systems development
- Facilitated workshops and exercises (e.g. strategising or team building)
- Conferences
- Roundtables
- Exposure visits/shadowing
- Internships
- Information sharing
- Collective learning
- Grants for capacity development
- Awareness raising (e.g. civic education, campaigns of voter awareness or rights awareness)

Less commonly used include:

- Facilitation of network/umbrella body development
- Civil society legislative and fiscal reform
- Building awareness and understanding of civil society within other sectors (public sector; local authorities; faith institutions; media; corporations etc)
- Resourcing joint cross-sector projects
- Investment in local civil society support capacity
- Development of codes of practice/ethical codes
- Support to development of resource mobilisation strategies
- OD process and change management consultancies

When choosing activities a critical consideration is whether the different types of activities can be done simultaneously, or sequentially.

For example, skills development could use a combination of activities such as face-to-face training, on the job training, and workplace mentoring. Will there be potential clashes between activities, will a certain staff level (for example project managers) in an organisation become overloaded, and how will this affect the rest of the organisation?

> **? Critical thoughts**
>
> Is the programme design in danger of undermining existing capacities once it is implemented?
>
> Will it incapacitate an organisation, even unintentionally, by the strategy and activities being too demanding or poorly designed?

Choosing appropriate activities according to the capacity building intervention level

Part Three, Chapter 6

Some activities particularly lend themselves to capacity building work at the level of the civil society sector as a whole, whilst others are more appropriate for capacity building at the level of individuals. Below are examples of activities associated with the levels of:

- Cross-sector
- Civil society sector-wide
- Sub-sector or networks
- Individual organisations

Cross-sector activities (CSOs, public sector, private sector, international aid sector etc)

Examples of activities:

- Facilitating forums, conferences, round tables
- Joint training
- Facilitating joint planning
- Building capacity for dialogue

The key feature of these activities is relationship building through joint discussion, debate and reflection. However, it may be appropriate to introduce activities which bring the sectors together for joint initiatives. This can also incorporate a dimension of reflection, for example on collaboration or relationship building. Such initiatives might include:

- Joint training on key capacity interests shared across sectors, for example, media training or environmental awareness.
- Making a number of training places available to participants from different sectors when relevant workshops take place, for example management training or fundraising.

> **◉ Case example**
>
> A civil society strengthening programme in Oman that involved strategic management training for civil society leaders. The training included a session on 'strategic relationships', for part of which Omani government officials were invited to participate. The group exercise of 'mapping' strategic relationships enabled the participants to explore common challenges about identifying and investing in relationships in a strategic manner, as well as sharing their views of how they saw each other in terms of importance and influence.

- Engaging in joint actions, which include an action–reflection element. For example, including a collaborative work project within a modular training programme.

> **◉ Case example**
>
> In Albania a social development project brought together local government officials and CSO representatives in a joint training programme. As part of the initiative, a number of concrete projects were identified which involved close collaboration across the two sectors. The training was implemented in modules, and an element of each module was a session dedicated to shared reflection on the progress of the projects.

Consider factors such as context and timing when designing cross-sector activities. Be guided by local stakeholders as to what is most appropriate in relation to political sensitivities and relationships. Bringing together government and CSOs too early in the programme may be counter-productive.

Sector wide activities (CSOs as a whole)

Examples of activities:

- Institutional development – support to umbrella bodies
- Strengthening capacity for self-assessment in order to define its development strategies.
- Civil society legislation and fiscal reform
- CSO forums
- Codes of Practice
- Support for NGO support organisations
- Building media awareness of the sector

These types of activities address the 'enabling environment'. These might include:

- Initiatives focused on the legal and/or fiscal regulations that affect the sector, for example tax reform so that CSOs can raise funds locally without being taxed.

> **◉ Case example**
>
> In Oman, a sector strengthening programme implemented by INTRAC and the International Programme of the UK Charity Commission (CC) aimed at supporting the development of the civil society sector by working simultaneously with both civil society and government, by:
>
> a) addressing shared capacity challenges by means of modular training programmes for the formally registered local NGOs (INTRAC)
>
> b) working with the Government to build an understanding of the sector, and review its legal regulatory framework (CC).
>
> The two implementing organisations regularly communicated with each other on the progress of the work.

- Strengthening the profile of the sector with the general public. This may include initiatives which promote the volunteer ethos; focus on building an understanding of the sector within the media; or support initiatives such as charity fairs or general public education on the role of the sector.
- The development of a published code of practice is another way to improve public accountability of CSOs.
- Efforts dedicated to strengthening the sector's capacity to analyse the environment in which it operates and identify issues to address.

Example of an analytical tool:

The ARVIN analytical framework looks at five key elements in the environment, each of which affect the capacity of the sector:

Association – the culture, political space, power etc for citizens to associate in organisational forms.

Resources – the diversity, origins, and sustainability of the resources necessary for effective association.

Voice – access, cost, infrastructure etc related to communication.

Information – access, control, ownership of information.

Negotiation – opportunities, culture, capacity to negotiate interests and conflicts.

The tool systematically focuses on questions within each element, in order to identify specific contextual characteristics. This can provide the basis for action plans to address the findings within each element.

(Source: World Bank, www.worldbank.org)

Other types of sector wide activities might be more focused on addressing the capacity issues *within the sector* as a whole. These may include:

- Support to CSO umbrella bodies.
- Investment in a locally sustainable support capacity provider for the sector.
- Establishment of national civil society development trusts or foundations, offering local grants for organisational strengthening, exchange visits, international linkages etc.
- Open training, inviting participants from all types of CSOs to participate jointly in courses designed to address common capacity challenges.

Sub-sector or network activities (groups of CSOs focused on thematic interests, geography, identity etc)

Examples of activities:

- Strengthening internal network functioning
- Communications skills development
- Supporting knowledge sharing initiatives
- Constituency building/resource mobilisation
- Facilitating platforms, for example poverty or HIV/AIDS
- Supporting the development of federations of community based organisations
- Building capacity for local government reform and participation
- Support to the development of policy shaping and influencing capacities
- Training in participatory budgeting (planning, monitoring public expenditure)

Organisations may come together based on common features in their form or function, or around plans of action, networks of learning or permanent coordinating bodies.

Specific activities focus particularly on relational and/or internal capacities as shown in the table alongside. These capacities are critical for ensuring effective and healthy sub-sector/network relationships.

Part One, Chapter 3

INTERVENTION STRATEGIES AND ACTIVITIES

Activities	Capacity indicator (1)	Capacity indicator (2)
Communications skills development.	Trust has been built between the network and outside bodies, by ensuring regular and effective communications.	All network members have access to a self-designed monthly newsletter via letter, email or post boards and opportunities to contribute regularly.
Carrying out an organisational review focused on strengthening internal governance and management.	The network governance body has a clearly defined role and its management responsibilities (if any) are known and understood by all member organisations.	The Secretariat Staff have written job descriptions which are known and understood by all member organisations.
Strengthening the constituency.	The constituency has been consulted in defining the role of the Board and Chair.	The constituency has regular opportunities to share their views about the future of the network.
Clarifying the role of the network Secretariat in relation to advocacy work.	All members are clear on the criteria to be used to decide when the network Secretariat is the primary 'advocacy agent' and when it is to play a more supporting role to the members' individual advocacy efforts.	The job descriptions of Secretariat staff indicate clearly the parameters for their engagement in direct advocacy initiatives.
Training of network leaders in conflict resolution skills.	Internal disputes amongst network members are quickly and effectively resolved.	Network leaders are respected and recognised as effective in resolving disputes between members.

Recently, much emphasis has been placed on providing technical support to increasing network capacities to shape public policy and monitor public expenditure. This is seen as key to ensuring effective civil society network engagement in the arenas of poverty reduction and democratisation. However, if carried out in isolation and without considering support to the internal and relational capacity areas, support of this nature may be limited. Ensuring effective internal functioning by supporting activities to clarify the identity, values and beliefs, member expectations and methods of working are all important dimensions of capacity building at this level.

Activities with individual organisations (for example intermediary NGOs, social movements, self help organisations and community based organisations)

Examples of activities:

- Organisational change processes
- Internal governance and leadership development programme management
- Systems development constituency building
- Relationship strengthening

Part One, Chapter 2 and Part Three, Chapter 6

Activities must be tailored to the individual type of organisation, based on an initial **capacity assessment** or **diagnosis** – a systematic process to identify the current capacity of an organisation. This is a crictical area, the key points on which are below.

The methods used vary in the degree to which they are participatory, and can be processes solely led by the organisation's own staff or ones which draw on the expertise of an external consultant (or a combination).

Selecting an appropriate approach (methods and tools) depends on:

- **Purpose** – for example a focused needs assessment as precursor to a training initiative, or a general check as part of ongoing capacity development.
- **Organisational complexity** – i.e. size, budget, breadth of objectives, diversity in resource base and relationship patterns. More complex is more likely to need tailor-made tools.
- **Cost** – including staff time.
- **Level of concern or crisis** – if severe, then it may be necessary to put effort and resources into an assessment process which may be out of proportion to the complexity of the organisation.
- **Degree of vulnerability** – where self-analysis is likely to be disturbing, it may be appropriate to start with a more superficial assessment method, slowly moving into sensitive areas once confidence is established.

The assessment may be against a particular set of capacities as identified by the answer to the 'capacity for what?' question. For example, where an organisation, through its strategic planning process, identifies the need to diversify its resource base, it needs to know the implications of this – what kind of capacities it will need in order to raise those resources and manage them. It can gather information about what other similar organisations have in place (**benchmarking**), but it will need to do an assessment of itself to identify weaker and stronger areas. The exact methods and tools it uses to do the assessment will be those most suited to obtaining the relevant information.

However, the organisation may want a more holistic picture – one which explores the capacity levels in all aspects of the 'to do', 'to be' and 'to relate' dimensions of the organisation. This may form part of a long-term organisational development (OD) process, which takes the organisation's identity and mission and purpose (the 'core' of the onion) as key reference points. It may use this as a benchmark for a locally appropriate definition of what an ideal or healthy organisation looks like. It will most probably imply the use of in-depth and diverse methods and tools.

Example of an Organisational Assessment prompt list

Here are nine key areas to consider before undertaking an assessment.

- **Why are you thinking of doing an Organisational Assessment?**
    - Who is initiating and owning it?
    - What is it for ?
    - What does it emerge from and feed into (capacity building or organisational development process)?

- **What is the scope of the OA?**
  - Is it organisation-wide or for a particular aspect/unit?
- **What approach will you take?**
  - 'Outside-in' i.e. referencing to some external point of comparison such as a benchmark
  - 'Inside-out' i.e. referencing to the organisation's own mission and strategic goals to see the degree of fit
- **Who will be involved?**
  - Is it a self-assessment, expert-led or a combination?
  - Will you use an internal task group? If so, what is its role and profile of members?
  - In decision-making?
- **Is the timing right and what resources have been made available?**
  - Have you identified the cost in terms of people's time, materials, events?
  - Do you have the expertise and skills available to you?
- **What methods and tools will you use that are appropriate to the organisation, context, culture, purpose and level of concern?**
  - Is there a shared understanding on organisations and their effectiveness?
  - What degree of complexity and how participatory in nature?
  - Are the indicators clear and measurable?
  - How will you gather and organise your data?
  - How are you addressing the need for 'triangulation'?
- **What kind of sensitivities, fears and resistance may emerge during the process?**
  - Are people prepared/motivated?
  - Influence of gender/power imbalances?
- **How will you manage the process?**
  - Communications, monitoring and evaluation, information/data storage, confidentiality, overall sponsor
- **What will the results look like?**
  - What kind of output/s

> **? Critical thoughts**
>
> Have you considered the full range of factors which may influence the choice of assessment method?
>
> Who has been involved in the selection or design of the tools? Does this include the organisations which will be using them?

Once the assessment has indicated the areas for development, then **select capacity building activities** appropriate to the desired improvements.

The pyramid model below illustrates a range of activities that tend to be used within organisational capacity building initiatives. It shows how often they are used (horizontal axis) and to what extent they contribute to deep change within the organisation (vertical axis).

Options for organisational support

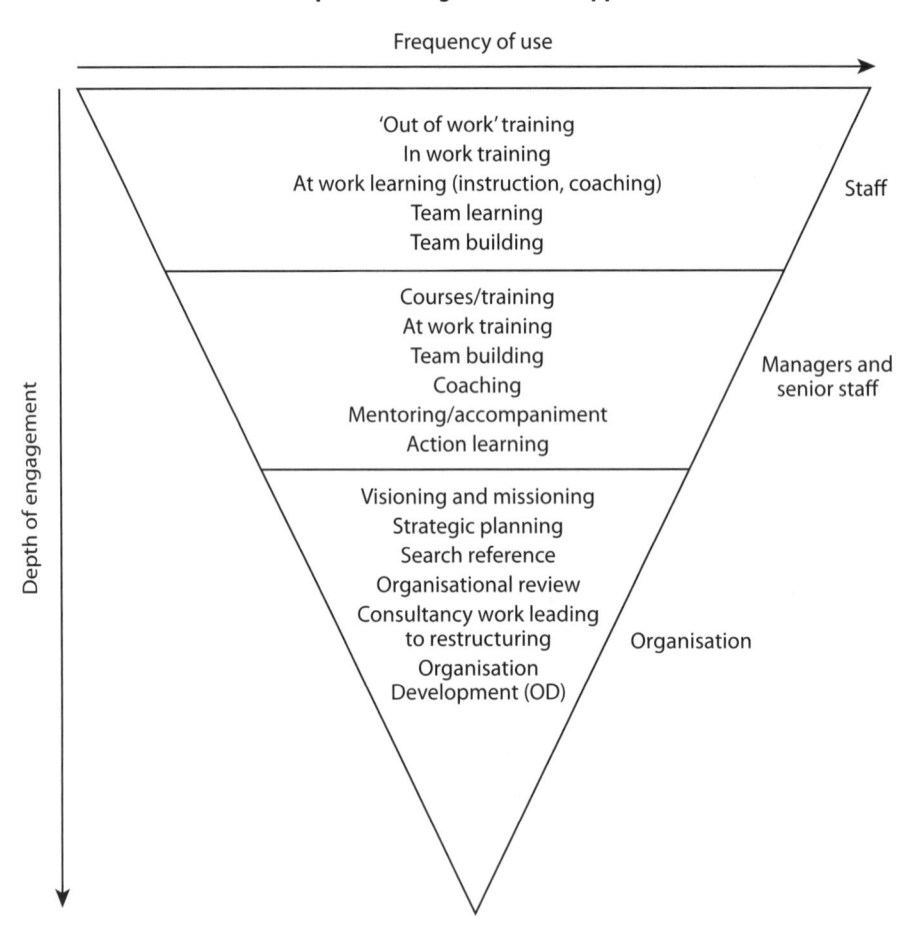

Frequency of use (horizontal axis, top)
Depth of engagement (vertical axis, left)

Staff:
- 'Out of work' training
- In work training
- At work learning (instruction, coaching)
- Team learning
- Team building

Managers and senior staff:
- Courses/training
- At work training
- Team building
- Coaching
- Mentoring/accompaniment
- Action learning

Organisation:
- Visioning and missioning
- Strategic planning
- Search reference
- Organisational review
- Consultancy work leading to restructuring
- Organisation Development (OD)

Source: INTRAC

For example, providing training at the individual level is the most common type of capacity building intervention. Change is focused on the individual developing skills, knowledge, attitudes and values to meet the needs of the job, team and organisation. However, it is generally considered to be the most superficial in terms of contribution to long-term and sustainable organisational change.

The next level is focused on team development, which is also frequently used. Activities at this level may include skills development linked to the introduction of new procedures, or improved communication through team building.

The next level moves into deeper organisation change. Capacity building across teams within an organisation, for example, can improve organisational learning by ensuring knowledge is shared and cross-fertilisation of ideas takes place.

Deeper still are capacity building activities that focus on the whole organisation – a range of options such as the development of human resource management strategies, organisational strategising, change management and organisation development.

In general, the deeper the change, the more complex and long-term the process. In practice, these capacity building interventions may work simultaneously or be part of the same capacity building strategy. This is when the change is likely to be most comprehensive.

Case example

A local NGO working with people living with HIV/AIDS wants to expand its operations and diversify its resource base away from dependence on one INGO partner. The implications include the need to develop leadership and management skills, review its formal registration and fiscal status, and network more regionally. Capacity building will be necessary at several levels:

- Skills development for staff teams in fundraising and regional networking.
- Inter-team development across the districts to provide an increased sense of working as one entity with common values and identity.
- Developing an organisation development plan, to include strategic planning and leadership development.
- Creating ongoing learning opportunities for staff and external stakeholders to prepare for the organisation's eventual independence.

In this example, the range of activities will form the overall capacity building strategy. Planning for implementation must consider the complementarities of each activity, the timeline for each activity, who will be involved, when and where activities will take place, resource implications and budget requirements.

Critical thoughts

How deep are you prepared to go in terms of organisational change? Can your programme contemplate engaging in major change interventions which cut to the 'core' of the onion?

Activities with grassroots CBOs (as a sub-group of the organisational level)

Examples of activities:

As with the organisational level but also:

Constituency building; membership recruitment/retention strategies; rights awareness training; negotiation skills training; strengthening capacity for community services provision

With CBOs, whilst many of the activities will be the same as working with other individual organisations, the way of working is different. It is critical that capacity building activities are relevant and suitable for community members.

Although strategic planning may not be necessary, developing strategic thinking skills could be useful. For example, it might not be appropriate to focus on strategic planning as a response to an identified weakness in strategic capacity. Another, more suitable approach to encourage development in this area might be to place greater emphasis on strategic *thinking* rather than offer training in how to produce a strategic plan. Similarly, the development of leadership and decision making skills appropriate to the community and cultural context must take into consideration the power dynamics within the community, amongst other factors.

There are some specific activities that are more suitable for organisational capacity building work with CBOs. In particular, due to their nature as grassroots membership organisations, it is necessary to pay particular attention to strengthening the 'rootedness' of the organisation in its community. Developing membership recruitment or retention strategies may also be an appropriate activity. Finally, strengthening negotiation skills may be another specific focus, given the increasing opportunities for CBO engagement with local authorities.

Part One, Chapter 3

Activities with individuals

Examples of activities:

- Literacy training
- Civic education
- Rights awareness raising
- Voter registration

Although there are some common capacity building activities most often used with individuals, such as training, mentoring and coaching, the purpose of the activity will vary considerably. For example, if the capacity building programme is to strengthen the broader civil society sector, activities targeted towards individuals may be concerned with raising awareness of civic rights or political issues. On the other hand if the programme focus is to strengthen a particular organisation, activities with individuals will vary according to the need of an organisation.

Factors affecting choice of strategies and activities

This chapter started by highlighting the need to consider a range of factors that will ultimately affect the choice of both strategies and activities of the programme. The following are questions to ask in relation to these factors:

- **Context**: what specific characteristics of the local, national and international context may influence the effectiveness of different types of activity? The implications might be that a certain type of activity might not be appropriate at a particular moment. For example, in a context of political instability, open and public activities like roundtables might be inappropriate. Where HIV/AIDS has a profound impact, an organisation development plan will need to anticipate how this might affect staff competencies. A useful tool to analyse the more general characteristics of the context is PESTLE. This is an environmental scanning instrument which looks at trends taking place in the political, economic, social, technological, legal and environmental factors areas – at local, national, regional or international levels.

⇔ Part Three, Chapter 3

- **Culture**: what specific cultural issues will affect the programme? What sub-cultures exist within the society in which the programme will be operating, (for example geographical, ethnic, identity based)? When working with organisations, how is culture expressed – for example, how things are done, traditions and values, and how does this affect or is affected by individuals? How will this influence the choice of appropriate activities or the way in which these may be delivered?

⇔ Part Three, Chapter 3

- **Timeframes**: who or what is driving the initiative? Who is setting the timeframes (for example, donors)? What are their deadlines and the implications for the design phase? For example, are they supporting short or longer term interventions? What are the implications for the choice of activities? For example, training is popularly used, but are there other activities, that may take longer but could be more effective – for example, on-the-job training, coaching and mentoring programmes.

- **Resources**: Are activities realistic given the programme's funding? Does the design phase of the programme have a budget? Are there sufficient people to work on the programme design and implementation?

⇔ Part Three, Chapter 8

- **Commitment**: Who are the programme 'champions'? What level of commitment exists, for example, time, knowledge and experience sharing, money, materials? Do activities rely on high commitment levels from a certain groups of individuals – do commitment levels match investment levels?

SUMMARY

This chapter highlighted the need to consider the factors that will affect the choice of both strategies and activities of the programme. These should be openly shared before the programme starts.

Stakeholders should be part of the design of strategies and activities if they are to be successfully implemented.

Intervention strategies and activities are the most visible and tangible elements of the overall programme. Key points include:

- When choosing strategies for the programme it is important to consider the effect of one strategy upon another, and choose those that complement each other.
- Some activities lend themselves to particular levels of capacity building work, whilst others are more generic in nature and can be utilised with all levels. It is important to consider which is appropriate to the level at which the programme is operating. A poorly designed strategy and range of activities which cannot be implemented due to other demands may incapacitate an organisation and individuals, even unintentionally.

RECOMMENDED READING

Fowler, A with Goold, L and James, R. *Participatory Self Assessment of NGO Capacity*, INTRAC, 1995

Gubbels, P and Koss, C. 'From the roots up: Strengthening Organisational Capacity through guided self-assessment'. World Neighbours Field Guide: Capacity Building, 2000

www.km4dev.org/journal, Vol.2 No.2 (2006). Special issue dedicated to capacity building for networks.

Ashman, D et al. *Supporting Civil Society Networks in International Development Programs*, AED Center for Civil Society & Governance, 2005

Crookes, B. *Working Without Words: Exploring the use of cartooning and illustration in organisational capacity building*. INTRAC, 2004

Chapter 5
Three common programming approaches

There are various options for the overall package of capacity building work. The 'legs' of the capacity building framework will vary in shape and size, just as human legs vary in appearance. This chapter explores three common approaches to shaping a capacity building programme, as promoted by sponsors of such initiatives:

- Civil society sector/sub-sector strengthening programmes
- Partner capacity building programmes
- Programmes emphasising long-term organisation development (OD) of individual organisations.

Programme shape

Within each of these approaches there are many variations. This chapter will not explore this diversity, but will focus on the broad similarities and differences across the three approaches, so that the reader gains a more general understanding.

1. Civil society sector/sub-sector strengthening programmes

These programmes tend to be sponsored primarily by official donor agencies and national governments. There are several reasons for this: it is potentially a huge investment in terms of cost and human resources; the operational scale and diversity of participants is very wide; and such initiatives quite often involve engagement with national governments, which may be harder for INGO actors to access.

Increasingly these programmes have been part of, or linked formally to, broader sectoral or thematic programmes, for example rural livelihoods, governance, peace building etc. Thus, very often the triggers of change are found in the political arena, in the shifts in trends in the international development sector and in the aid architecture.

> **Case example: Cypriot Civil Society Strengthening Programme (CCSSP)**
>
> 'Against a background of division and suspicion, social development in Cyprus relies on building trust and cooperation between the Greek Cypriot and Turkish Cypriot communities of the island. The promotion of citizens' activities and contacts outside of formal politics helps to this end: through the Cyprus Civil Society Strengthening Programme, UNDP helps civil society groups from both communities work together for concrete goals and to develop their role in the democratic governance of the island.' (UNDP-ACT, www.undp-act.org)
>
> The CCSSP has the following objectives:
>
> - Develop the skills of individual leaders, staff and volunteers to improve conceptual understanding and practical skills in a number of key areas.
> - Develop organisations' knowledge and skills in designing, planning and managing their own organisational development processes.
> - Increase capacity of CSOs to develop broader and stronger relationships with each other, inter-communally, and with authorities and policy makers, and raise the visibility and profile of the sector as a whole.
> - Develop local trainers', consultants', and CSOs' capacity and skills to design and develop appropriate capacity assessment and development plans.
> - Increase debate, knowledge and understanding of key issues facing civil society, through dialogue within and outside civil society.
>
> The CCSSP is structured around a range of complementary interventions:
>
> i) Open training courses
>
> ii) Tailor-made technical assistance
>
> iii) Long-term capacity building
>
> iv) Dialoguing events.
>
> These components form the guiding framework for delivery of the CCSSP, each contributing to one or more of the programme's objectives.

Implications for the INGO or national support providers

Often these programmes are contracted out using a competitive bidding process. The donor agency will usually manage these in two phases – a tender for the initial mapping and design work and then a subsequent tender for the programme implementation. Increasingly these programmes are operated by private sector consultancy firms, possibly in conjunction with INGOs. Where the programme initiative is sponsored by official donor agencies (for example bilateral agencies, UNDP, EU, World Bank etc) and an INGO or local support provider is contracted as the implementer, the following should be considered:

1. What are the values and agendas behind the programme? Is there a fit between the values of the donors and implementers/support providers? Are there any foreseeable tensions that may arise because of different agendas held by diverse stakeholders? How will these be managed?

↔ Part Two, Chapters 6 and 7

2. How much scope is there to influence the parameters of the programme, throughout all the stages of design and implementation? Are some of these more critical than others? For example, is the timeframe set by the donors/sponsors a realistic one in relation to the objectives and the methods being proposed?

3. Is the size of the implementing organisation appropriate to the scale of the work? If not, then what alliances or ways of working will ensure appropriate resourcing?

↔ Part Two, Chapters 6 and 7

4. How prepared is the organisation for managing complexity, for example, the range of relationships and organisations involved? Does the implementing organisation have the expertise required to work on change processes at diverse levels – individuals, organisational, sector and societal – and make connections across them?

5. Do the proposed evaluation/impact assessment methodology and indicators fit with the organisation's own evaluation process? Performance measurement is particularly challenging when dealing with capacity building at this level.

↔ Part Three, Chapter 8

6. How will ownership by CSO participants be achieved? Is this an exercise being introduced by donors as a 'hoop' through which they must jump in order to get funding for their programmes of work?

↔ Part Three, Chapters 1 and 2

> **? Critical thoughts**
>
> Have you thought through all the implications of engaging in capacity building at this level?
>
> Are you involved in peer exchange, learning communities or other knowledge-based efforts to share reflections on the critical challenges of working at capacity building at this level?

These questions are still relevant in cases where the initiative is coming from the civil society sector. The preparation of proposals for grants for sector-level capacity building must consider the full range of issues identified above.

2. Partner capacity building programmes

This approach is mostly used by larger INGOs or other international organisations who work through partnerships. It may take the form of initiatives targeted at strategic partners i.e. focused on organisations with whom there is a long-term relationship based on shared values, mission compatibility etc. Alternatively partner capacity building may be time-bound i.e. for the duration of a strategic plan which emphasises a particular sector or theme within which organisations must fit, if they are to be considered as partners.

⮂ Part Two, Chapter 4

The capacity building methods used vary. For example, it is more likely that within a strategic partner capacity building programme there would be more emphasis on a holistic approach, and a concern to ensure sustainability and a healthy organisation. This is most likely to reflect the intrinsic approach to capacity building which emphasises robust capacity.

Capacity building work in a context of partnerships forged around shared thematic interests or working towards the same strategic objective might emphasise the capacity areas of the 'to do' dimension more. The approach is more likely to focus on strengthening capacities for programme performance and delivery as well as those needed for effective upwards accountability (project reporting, financial management etc). This case is a more functional approach to capacity building. In both approaches, clarity of purpose and identification of capacity change objectives are critical.

⮂ Part One, Chapter 1 and Part Three, Chapters 3 and 4

The parameters for the design and implementation of a partner capacity building approach tend to be set by the sponsoring organisation's organisational imperatives and strategy. The scale of such programmes depends on the number of partners, but normally would not be too large. The costs would tend to be relatively low, possibly with less emphasis on individual tailor-made interventions and more emphasis on the shared capacity issues that can be addressed through collective activities. Where there is tailor-made support provided to individual partners, sponsoring organisations commonly develop capacity assessment tools that reflect their interests, perhaps emphasising certain capacity areas above others.

> ### 👁 Case example
>
> INGO Kids in Action (KIA) is focused on children's well-being. It has recently produced a new corporate strategic plan in response to shifts in official donor policies and a review of its role in development. This has several implications:
>
> - changing from its previous mix of partner funding and its own service delivery and advocacy work.
> - consultation with partners across the regions to identify the 'value-added' it makes within the partnership relationship.

- the need to drastically reduce the scale of its service delivery operations, and restrict them to specific contexts such as conflict or natural disasters.

In addition to reviewing its role, the organisation has also undertaken a thematic focusing exercise. As a result, there are now just three broad objectives which will be expressed through global thematic programmes:

- increasing children's access to primary school education
- ensuring the well-being of children orphaned as a result of HIV/AIDS
- ensuring the rights of children are respected in the context of conflict-affected environments

This new framework means developing exit strategies for some of the previous work and partnerships that no longer meet the new strategic priorities.

In this context KIA is initiating a new partner capacity building programme, which will cross-cut the three thematic programmes. Eventually, KIA hopes to develop a capacity building policy to provide guidance on the principles, concepts and approaches to be used by each country team. It is not able to proceed with this until the organisation has completed the restructuring of the headquarters team which works on cross-organisational methodological and programme policy development. KIA hopes to recruit a capacity building specialist to work as a member of the new team.

In the interim, the senior management have asked each country programme to develop a partner capacity building strategy, based on in-country dialogues. Each country will review its partner portfolio in the light of the new corporate strategies, which means undertaking three different kinds of dialogues:

1. With partners who no longer fit with the new KIA priorities, the team will identify capacity development needs that could be responded to as part of an exit strategy to be implemented over the next two years;

2. With existing partners whose mission and programme focus does currently cover some or all of the aspects of the three themes, KIA will identify the capacity development needs with regard to new future challenges. These would form the core of the partner capacity building dimension within each of the thematic programmes operating in that country.

3. As the KIA country team identifies potential new partners, the staff will discuss the 'value-added' that KIA can provide in the relationship, with capacity building likely to form a key element of that contribution.

The KIA leadership recognise that their staff face many challenges in undertaking this task. There are very few field based staff who have had experience of capacity building work and no existing organisational guidelines to help the field teams develop their strategies. However, senior management are forced to make this request of their country programmes, as they need to ensure that the capacity building dimension of the thematic programmes is identified in time to be included in the new major grant proposals being developed as a response to the changing funding climate. They have however, decided to incorporate a strong learning dimension to the first year of the new thematic programmes, with a view to capturing the lessons from engaging in this new approach and building on the successes. These lessons will then be incorporated into the new policy and guidelines for the partner capacity building work.

Implications for INGOs and their partners

There are a number of key considerations when embarking upon partner capacity building initiatives, including:

1. What role will the staff from the sponsoring INGO play? If actively engaged in the delivery of capacity building services, how will this be affected by the donor role that the INGO also plays?

    ⇄ Part Three, Chapter 7

2. Will the funding sources limit the way in which capacity building is practiced? How far is the INGO prepared to compromise the good practice principles it aspires to?

3. In the case of strategic partners, who is setting the capacity building agenda? Key power and partnership issues must be considered here.

    ⇄ Part Two, Chapter 4

4. In the case of other partners, is the power dynamic transparent? Is the INGO clearly communicating about how capacity building priorities are being set and how they relate to its own programme imperative? This is particularly true when identifying the capacity areas to be addressed, i.e. the answer to the 'capacity for what?' question.

5. How will the INGO approach the learning dimension of the capacity building work? Is it shaping the initiative around an understanding of two-way capacity building which implies an investment in its own capacity to learn and change?

    ⇄ Part Two, Chapter 5

3. Organisation Development (OD)

This approach focuses on the long-term, self-managed change process that individual organisations may choose.

⇄ Part One, Chapter 2 and Part Three, Chapter 4, pyramid diagram

Some definitions of OD include:

> 'The applied behavioural science discipline that seeks to improve organisations through planned, systematic, long range efforts focused on the organisation culture and its human and social processes.'
> (Beckhard and Harris, 1987)

> 'The facilitation of an organisation's capacity to self-reflect, self-regulate and take control of its own processes of improvement and learning.'
> (Kaplan, 1996)

'Organisational development is … a planned change that aims to increase the organisation's capacity for learning, awareness and self-understanding, so that the organisation becomes better equipped to take control over its situation, activities and future.'
(Swedish Mission Council, 2002)

As a discipline, Organisation Development (OD) originated in the USA in the 1960s, but its roots can be traced back as far as the 1930s. OD as a term is generally very widely and loosely used. There is no one definition of OD which all adhere to. OD is often used to describe an intervention which might be more accurately called an OD consultancy as consultancy is the prime intervention to be used. People tend to use these words synonymously, which can create confusion.

Expanding on the definitions above, INTRAC understands that any OD intervention should have significant elements of the following:

Ten core ingredients of Organisation Development

- The goal of OD is not just that an organisation can deal with its current problems today, but that it can be strengthened to address its future problems.
- OD aims to develop an organisation's capacity to manage change and learn from its own practice.
- OD sees organisations as whole systems of interrelated components, and therefore the importance of understanding the 'whole picture' of the organisation in its environment.
- OD uses a process of collaborative diagnosis of the key issues by the key stakeholders, to maintain ownership of the issues identified and the process.
- OD stresses senior management commitment and support to the whole process.
- OD looks at the cultural and political dimensions of organisations and change, not just the technical.
- OD is about conscious not accidental change.
- OD focuses on people, not just physical resources.
- OD is a long term process, not one-off or quick fix.
- OD focuses on enabling the organisation to become more effective in carrying out its mission through the development of an appropriate and effective organisational practice and culture.

Source: Adapted from James, R. *Demystifying Organisational Development*, INTRAC, 1998

There are other organisational interventions, which in and of themselves would not fit our descriptions of OD, for example management skills training, or advice on finance systems. These are important capacity building interventions, which may be part of an OD process (if they were identified by the organisation through their own assessment as being critical), but if used in isolation would not fit with our definition.

CAPACITY BUILDING FRAMEWORK

OD can be usefully thought of as a process that goes through a series of stages. This process is sometimes called the **OD Cycle** and comprises, broadly, of six stages:

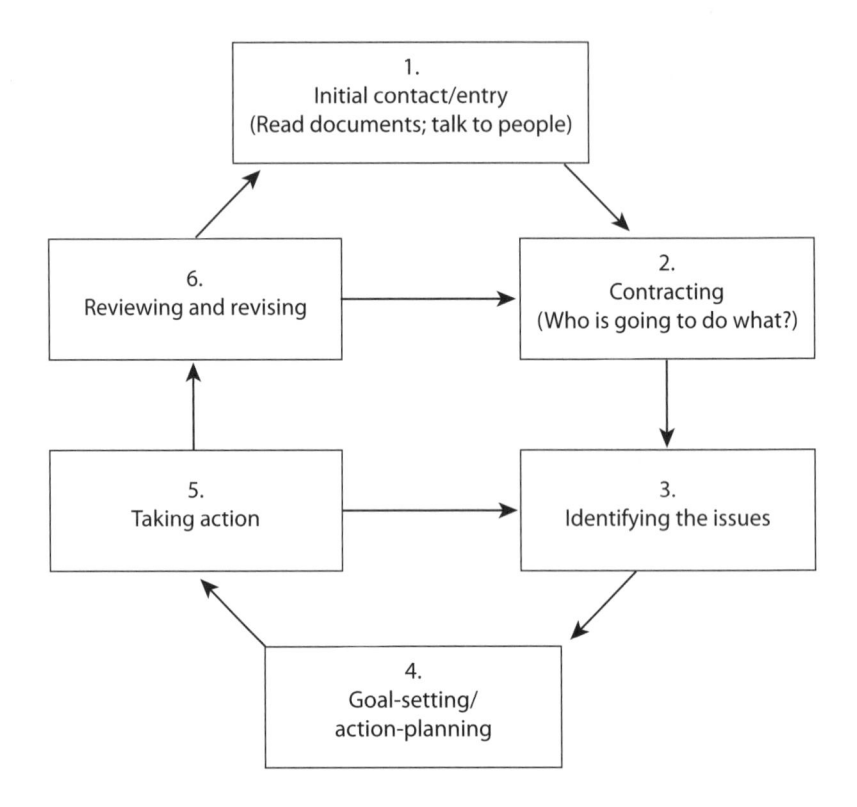

```
        1.
        Initial contact/entry
        (Read documents; talk to people)
              │
    ┌─────────┘
    │
    6.                          2.
    Reviewing and revising ───► Contracting
    ▲                           (Who is going to do what?)
    │                               │
    │                               ▼
    5.                          3.
    Taking action ─────────────► Identifying the issues
    ▲                               │
    │                               │
    └──────── 4. ◄──────────────────┘
             Goal-setting/
             action-planning
```

1. **Initial contact/entry** involves opening the relationship between the change agent and the organisation. It is at this stage that the viability of an OD intervention is tested.

2. **Contracting** involves developing a written agreement about what will be done and who will take responsibility. Most change agents agree that problems during an OD intervention can usually be traced back to poor initial contracting.

3. **Identifying the issues**. This involves collecting and analysing information in order to identify the key organisational issues. It requires sensitivity to the informal aspects of the organisation such as values, culture and power relations as well as the more formal such as organisational structure, systems and policies. Change agents may play a range of roles from reflector to advocate in order to help the organisation identify its own issues.

4. **Goal setting/action planning** involves generating and assessing options; deciding on priorities and gaining acceptance and commitment to address them. The issue of ownership of the process of change is crucial to the success of OD interventions. It can be useful at this stage to establish a representative steering group to guide and support the process of change.

5. **Taking action** involves anticipating the unintended as well as the intended consequences of the action; identifying forces that may resist or support change and devising a strategy to work with these forces. A commonly used strategy is to ensure

early successes by prioritising specific initiatives that can be achieved relatively easily. This gives confidence to those involved and sends a signal to others in the organisation that change is achievable and has tangible benefits.

6. **Reviewing and revising.** It is important for all of those involved with the OD intervention to be aware of the effects (intended and unintended) that it is having on the organisation. Opportunities for regular reflection on progress can provide valuable lessons for the organisation. If new information comes to light or important changes are happening outside the organisation, these may need to be factored in to the plans. Regular reviews of the intervention should be built in to the process and the feedback used to redefine the issues, if required.

OD is not a common approach, but it is one which most explicitly focuses on investing in the long term sustainability of individual CSO actors, and takes as its starting point an intrinsic approach which emphasises robust capacity. The strong emphasis on the importance of ownership by the CSOs involved means that it is the participating organisations that set the parameters and the pace. It may be resource intensive in terms of the demands on staff of the participant CSOs but less demanding on the promoting/sponsoring organisation. At times it may feel very 'inward looking' – the link with the programme work may appear weak, especially the link with making a difference to poor people's lives (in the case of a poverty reduction agenda for example).

Part One, Chapters 2 and 4 and Part Three, Chapter 2

Implications of working with an OD approach

The organisation sponsoring a capacity building programme that uses an OD approach must carefully consider these implications:

1. It is often very difficult to identify funders for this approach – so is your organisation prepared to use some of its own funds for this work?
2. Is your organisation ready to let go of the control – embrace the power issues that arise when engaging in this kind of approach?
3. The implications of doing so are that the change process is not controlled by project timelines nor designed around outcomes that have been predefined by the sponsoring INGO/donor.
4. It is inappropriate for staff of an organisation that is funding the CSO to be involved in the capacity building delivery in this approach.
5. It would be advisable to incorporate a dimension to the programme which invests in the strengthening of local capacity building support provision – for example via investing in local civil society support organisations. This is a critical factor in ensuring a sustainable approach and long-term quality support.

Key similarities and differences across the three approaches

The key similarities and differences in the characteristics of the three common approaches to capacity building can be summarised as:

		Organisation Development	Partner capacity building	Civil society strengthening
1	Framework for analysis	Organisational system or three circles model, with an emphasis on the internal functioning of the organisation (onion model) ⇔ Part One, Chapter 2	Three circles model or often focus is solely on the programme dimension. ⇔ Part One, Chapter 2	Concentric circles ⇔ Part Two, Chapter 4
2	Boundaries for engagement	Clear – within the organisation	Clear – between partners, but potentially unclear if understanding of partnership is not explicit	Unclear – depends on definition of civil society
3	Proximity to change in poor people's lives	Distant	Potentially close – focus is on performance and delivery	Difficult to attribute – change is over a long period of time
4	Ownership	By the organisation	Depends on who sets agenda for 'capacity building for what?'	Mainly donors and governments
5	Scale/number of participants	Relatively small (Board and staff)	Medium (with a set of partners)	Very large numbers, multiple stakeholders
6	Cost	Cost of leadership and staff time; cost of external facilitation	Potentially cost effective for all organisations	Potentially huge investment
7	Timeframes	Loose timeframes, depends on organisational need; ranges from short-term to ongoing	Majority are project based interventions; often depends on donor/back donor timeframes	Usually projects/programmes of three to five years
8	Intensity of engagement (who sets the pace?)	Organisation sets the pace, often can be very intensive for staff and leadership	Pace is set by project framework, time and resources available	Pace is variable and depends on timeframe. Can be a wide range of projects running simultaneously
9	Facilitators	Internal or third party change agent	External agents – local and international; donor/INGO partner	International consultants, private sector, governments and multinational institutions
10	Impact on immediate actors	Seen and felt within the organisation	On the participating organisations and relationship/s	On individuals and relationships; space for voice and engagement etc
11	Triggers of change	Often an organisational crisis	Sector or policy shifts	Political agendas

SUMMARY

This chapter explored three different approaches to shaping a capacity building programme:

- Civil society sector/sub-sector strengthening programmes
- Partner capacity building programmes
- Programmes emphasising long-term OD of individual organisations

It highlights the similarities and differences between each of the approaches and asks the reader some critical questions in relation to the most appropriate approach for their capacity building work. Key points include:

- Civil society/sector strengthening programmes require a certain level of resourcing, such as funding and experience in larger scale programmes. It requires a clear fit between agenda, values and principles to facilitate the development of such programmes.
- Partner capacity building programmes need to examine the role of staff from the sponsoring INGO. If actively engaged in the delivery of capacity building services, how will this be affected by the donor role that the INGO also plays and how may it compromise the good practice principles associated with quality capacity building?
- Organisation Development programmes require letting go of the control and encompassing the power issues that arise. For example, the change process is not controlled by project timelines or designed around donor/sponsor predefined outcomes and it is inappropriate for staff of an organisation that is funding the CSO to be involved in the capacity building delivery.
- It is advisable to incorporate a dimension to the programmes which invests in the strengthening of local capacity building support provision – for example via investing in local civil society support organisations. This is critical to ensuring a sustainable approach and long-term quality support.

RECOMMENDED READING

Civil society sector capacity building:

Fletcher Tembo, F and Wells, A with Sharma, B, Mendizaba, E. *Multi-donor support to civil society and engaging with 'non-traditional' civil society - A light-touch review of DFID's Portfolio*. ODI, 2007

ECDPM. *Institutional Development: Learning by Doing and Sharing – approaches and tools for supporting institutional development*. Draft booklet

Organisational Development:

Beckhard, R and Harris, R. *Organizational Transitions: Managing Complex Change*. Addison-Wesley, 1987

Frame, R, Hess, R and Kielsen, W. *The OD Source Book: A Practitioner's Guide*. University Associates, Inc, 1982

Garbutt, A. 'Civil Society Strengthening in Practice', in *Changing Expectations? The Concept and Practice of Civil Society in International Development*, INTRAC, 2003

James, R. *Demystifying Organisation Development: Practical Capacity Building Experiences of African NGOs*, INTRAC, 1998

Lipson, B. 'Identifying the Challenges of Capacity Building at Civil Society Level' in *Changing Expectations? The Concept and Practice of Civil Society in International Development*, INTRAC, 2003

Chapter 6
Support provision and roles

Capacity building programming will require clear decisions about how support will be made available to participating CSOs. This chapter focuses on the role of the 'sponsoring organisation' in the provision of such support. 'Sponsoring organisation' refers to actors involved in promoting a capacity building initiative, who may or may not be providing the funds for the work (frequently INGOs). This chapter begins by providing an overview of supply and demand issues; explores the spectrum of roles available to those who are sponsoring capacity building programmes, including a best practice model; and presents the critical factors to be considered when making choices about the roles to be played.

Programme shape

> **? Critical thought**
>
> It is important to step back and take a holistic view of your role in the capacity building process, both your role in the provision of capacity building support and in stimulating the demand for it.

↔ Part Two, values

An overview of supply and demand

A variety of data will be available to assist in the process of deciding on the most appropriate roles for the capacity building sponsor. The design process will have established:

- an understanding of the programming concept
- a contextual analysis of the sector and area or region
- a mapping and analysis of civil society capacity issues
- the goal and objectives for the capacity building initiative, and the links between these and the overarching agenda for engaging in such work
- the scope and levels of intervention, including the identification of which CSOs will be participating in the initiative
- the strategies and activities appropriate for the context and participating CSOs
- the timeframe for the initiative.

Such a thorough design process should reveal, for example, the current status of capacity building support and provision in the area or region where the programme will be running, the extent to which capacity building is understood and practised, and the knowledge and experience of local capacity building providers.

The following model provides an overview of both the supply and demand and illustrates some of the roles for both sides. There are four key groups involved in the supply and demand of capacity building:

a) the **client**, most often local CSOs, who in order to gain support for their capacity building needs will have two options, either to go to:

b) a local or regional/international **capacity building services provider** or to:

c) a capacity building **sponsor**, most often an INGO or partner organisation of the local CSO. In some cases such sponsors will also be providers, taking on a dual role.

d) In addition, some sponsors are also **donors**, directly funding capacity building initiatives themselves or obtaining back donors' support. The official agencies themselves, as well as providing back donor funding, also fund their own civil society capacity building programmes.

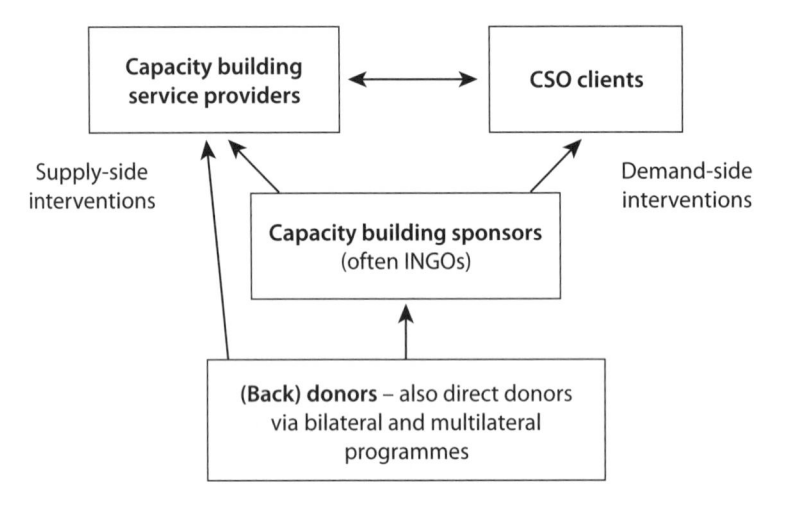

```
        ┌──────────────────┐                    ┌──────────────┐
        │ Capacity building│ ◄──────────►       │ CSO clients  │
        │ service providers│                    │              │
        └──────────────────┘                    └──────────────┘
Supply-side                                              Demand-side
interventions          ┌──────────────────────┐          interventions
                       │ Capacity building    │
                       │ sponsors (often INGOs)│
                       └──────────────────────┘
                                 ▲
                       ┌──────────────────────┐
                       │ (Back) donors – also │
                       │ direct donors via    │
                       │ bilateral and multi- │
                       │ lateral programmes   │
                       └──────────────────────┘
```

Source: Adapted from Springfield Centre for Looking at Business Support Services.

Stimulating demand

One of the activities of a capacity building sponsor will be to stimulate the demand for capacity building with partners or within the civil society sector in general. The next table highlights a number of options to consider as a sponsor:

Options for stimulating demand	How (activities)	Risk assessment
Raising awareness of what capacity building is	• awareness training • introductory workshops • access to information, for example books, documents, internet etc.	Low risk, can be done with relatively new partner relationships.
Raising awareness of potential capacity building providers	• informal and formal introductions • sharing information • sourcing or setting up a database of local providers.	Medium risk, requires good local capacity building providers.
Providing funding for capacity building	• funding partner's budget lines for capacity building • setting up internal capacity building fund which reacts to specific requests from partners • a combination of both of the above • voucher schemes where partners are given capacity building vouchers to use with dedicated capacity building providers.	Low to medium risk depending on relationships. Medium to high risk but can be high returns for stimulating demand.
Discussing, dialoguing and negotiating with partners about capacity building needs	Both parties share strengths and potential areas for improvement.	High risk, feasible in a healthy, mature, relationship. If not, may become directive and hands on.
Triggering a crisis	Withholding or removing funding to a partner may force the partner to seek capacity building support and therefore can be potentially developmental.	High risk, overt use of power which is not recommended. However it is practiced by frustrated donors (official and INGOs).
Cooperation and consistency amongst donor group/s on capacity building issues	Sending consistent messages about the need for capacity building within a sector and the most appropriate types of capacity building interventions.	Low risk, but requires time investment.

Try to mainstream discussions on capacity issues throughout your ongoing programme work. This means that you will constantly be exploring with partners the capacity implications of all programme initiatives you undertake together.

↪ Part Three, Chapter 1

The supply of capacity building services

Evidence suggests that providing capacity building support is most likely to be the focus of a capacity building programme, as opposed to stimulating demand for it. There are a number of different roles that can be played when supplying this support, and choosing the most appropriate roles will depend on the factors below. One of the important principles for a capacity building sponsor to consider when deciding on roles is to what extent they will have a 'hands-on' or 'hands-off' role.

- **Financing capacity building initiatives with no conditions**

The most hands-off role is funding with no strings attached. This is most likely to happen during a long-term relationship, or if this approach was considered to be in the best interests of the recipients and formed part of the working values and principles of the donor.

- **Financing capacity building initiatives through capacity building grant schemes**

This is a popular role, whereby certain pre-defined conditions or objectives are set by the grantor. Grantees adhere to funding conditions and submit reports. External evaluations may take place as a condition of the grantor.

- **Financing capacity building initiatives linked to third party capacity building providers**

De-linking the funding role and direct capacity building provision role, whilst dependant on a range of local conditions, is viewed as a best practice role. This is discussed further in the next section.

- **Acting as knowledge broker**

Providing information, contacts etc regarding capacity building initiatives. Signposting sources of support.

- **Facilitating capacity building activities**

Being involved in exchange visits, exposure initiatives, peer exchanges etc.

- **Delivering capacity building interventions**

Providing training and technical assistance, facilitating workshops, or carrying out organisational assessments.

- **Accompanying throughout capacity building interventions**

The most hands-on role – accompanying, coaching, partnering, modelling etc.

A recent INGO survey indicated a strong emphasis on direct capacity building implementation. The most common primary roles carried out by INGO staff were: designing the overall approach, making funding decisions and direct delivery of support services. On the other hand, signposting capacity building information and contacts was considered a primary role by only three per cent of organisations. This pie chart illustrates a range of principal roles undertaken by INGO staff:

Pie chart

- Monitoring and reporting on capacity building work 4.46%
- Providing information and contacts related to topics covered within capacity building initiatives 4.46%
- Other 6.7%
- Contracting support services for local CSOs (e.g. local consultants) 6.7%
- Providing advice or coaching to participants 11.16%
- Delivery of support directly to local CSOs (e.g. training/facilitating workshops) 17.71%
- Designing the overall approach 24.4%
- Deciding on funding of capacity building initiatives 24.4%

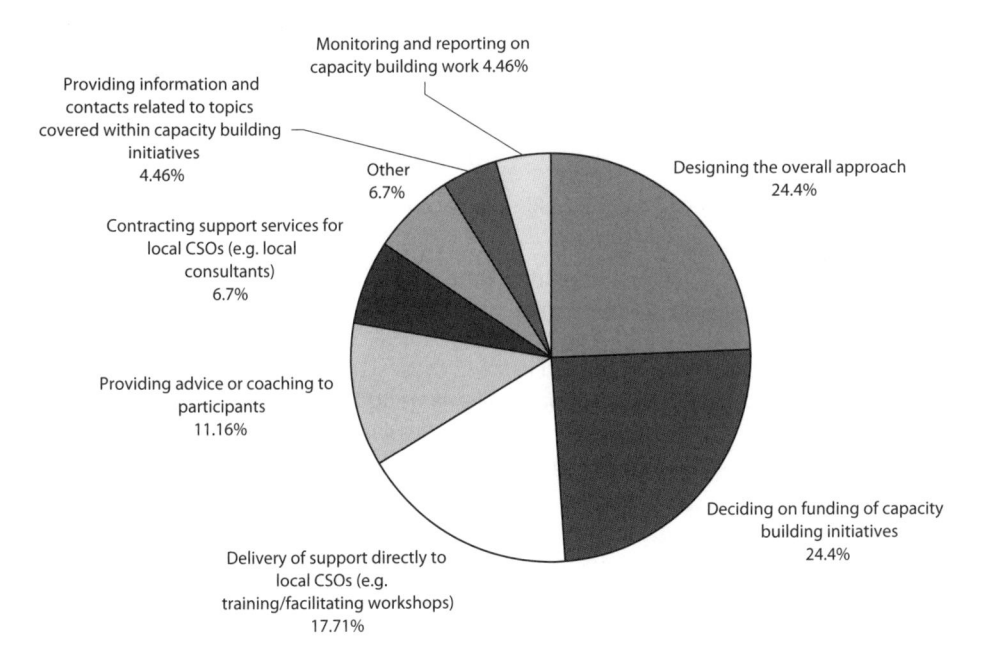

Source: Lipson, B and Warren, H. 'Taking stock', INTRAC, 2006

Evidence suggests that INGOs use a mixture of roles but tend to favour the more hands-on approach. If they are also funding the programme work of the CSOs, there is a risk that the funding will undermine ownership of the capacity building initiative. The result is often cosmetic or superficial changes. If, for example, CSO capacity building needs are concerned with more sensitive areas such as identity, leadership or strategic direction, then the presence of the funder of resources will be more likely to influence or even manipulate the process However, if, for example, capacity building interventions are at a more technical level such as financial management or computer literacy, then such a dual role is less problematic.

Part Three, Chapter 4

Sponsors of capacity building initiatives may also take on a range of supply roles and depending on the context and culture, may decide a more hands-on or hands-off role is most appropriate. Although taking on such an approach provides flexibility, it will not provide consistency. This could contribute to conceptual uncertainty if there are no clear guidelines established to indicate the circumstances which are influencing the sponsor to be more, or less, hands-on.

> ### Critical thoughts
>
> It could be argued that direct engagement of INGO staff in the delivery of capacity building services has become the new operational form, replacing the traditional service delivery in fields such as health, education and agriculture which is now undertaken more by local NGOs and CBOs.
>
> Does this apply to you or your organisation?

The 'best practice' role

Despite the variety of roles that can be played during the implementation of a capacity building programme, evidence suggests there is a two-fold best practice approach:

1. enable local ownership by de-linking capacity building service provision from the general funding relationship
2. supporting the development of local support providers thus contributing to more local and sustainable CSO capacity building.

The first point has been highlighted in other chapters of the book and is about being considered a 'developmental donor' or even a 'good donor'. Power is the underlying issue here, as once a funder becomes directly involved in capacity building, then the ownership of the capacity building programme can become undermined.

> Part Three, Chapters 1 and 2 and Part Two, Chapter 2

The support of local capacity building providers will ensure that local capacity is built and local providers become increasingly effective in providing services. Such local providers may include local NGO support organisations, training organisations, individual consultants sympathetic to the values of CSOs, and university departments. Capacity building sponsors can work with such providers in a number of ways:

- **Subsidising local capacity building providers**

Charging full cost recovery fees for capacity building services may not be feasible in all CSO sectors, especially in emerging sectors with small organisations are small and limited budgets. Furthermore, for capacity building providers to offer high quality services, investment in systematic organisational learning is required, the costs of which may not be possible to pass on to clients.

- **Contracting with local providers**

This approach can stimulate demand for local capacity building services and can enable a local provider to be more demand or market driven. However, just as contracting with CSOs and NGOs, care needs to be taken not to distort the market which needs to be CSO client-led rather than donor-led.

- **Capacity building with local providers**

If there are identified gaps in the provision of local capacity building services then in the long term it would be sustainable to build the capacity of a variety of local providers. Identifying relevant experiences and approaches to support provision elsewhere, facilitating exchanges and information provision are some of the ways in which a sponsor can facilitate this process. All of the good practice capacity building principles would apply in this work, as it does in the support to the capacity development of local CSOs in general.

- **Creating local capacity building providers**

Where there is no local capacity building provision, it may be possible for a sponsor to consider stimulating the formation of individuals and independent organisations to supply the sector with the required services. Providing links and contacts with providers in other countries will be a critical factor in ensuring that the sponsor is not unduly influencing the nature of the emerging local provision.

Choosing the optimal roles

Capacity building sponsors will always find a rationale for direct hands-on engagement. The reality is such that there is likely to be a need for a mix of roles, thus it is important for the sponsor to make clear decisions about which role is most appropriate. The table below illustrates the criteria for assessing the most appropriate capacity building role.

Criteria for assessing your capacity building role	Questions for assessing your capacity building role
1. Values fit	How far is your choice of roles reflecting the values of your organisation?
2. Good practice	How far are you considering the good practice of de-linking funding relationships from engagement in capacity building services?
3. Appropriateness	Have you considered which roles are appropriate for you to undertake in relation to the participating CSOs' context, type of organisation, length of relationship with you, phase of the capacity building programme etc?
4. Feasibility	What is feasible for your organisation to get engaged with? Do you have the right skills set, resource levels, knowledge etc to be in a position to play the roles you have selected?
5. Organisational imperative	How far is your choice based on a broader imperative for your organisation? For example, is a choice to engage in direct delivery being made to justify staffing levels? How clear are you on the value added that your staff are providing by being involved in hands-on as opposed to providing other types of support?

SUMMARY

This chapter focuses on the role of the sponsoring organisation in providing capacity building support. It covers an overview of supply and demand issues; explores the spectrum of roles available to those who are sponsoring capacity building programmes; and the critical factors to be considered when making choices about the role/s to be played. Key points include:

- There are four key groups involved in the supply and demand of capacity building: the **client**; a local or regional/international **capacity building services provider**; a capacity building **sponsor**, which may also provide support services as well as play the role of **donor**.

- One of the activities of a capacity building sponsor will be to stimulate the demand for capacity building with partners or within the civil society sector in general.
- One of the important principles for a capacity building sponsor to consider when deciding on roles, is to what extent they will have a hands-on or hands-off role. INGOs in particular mix various roles, with a tendency to the more hands-on approach. If they are also involved in funding the programme work of the participating CSOs, then that funding link is likely to undermine authentic ownership of the capacity building initiative.

A best practice approach is twofold: enabling local ownership by de-linking capacity building service provision from the general funder relationship, and supporting the development of local support providers to contribute to more local and sustainable CSO capacity building.

RECOMMENDED READING

Lipson, B, and Warren, H. 'Taking stock: a snapshot of INGO engagement in civil society capacity building', Conference paper, INTRAC, December 2006

PACT. 'Building Dynamic Local Service Provider Communities – a Value Chain Approach'. Available at www.impactalliance.org

Chapter 7
Resourcing a capacity building programme

This chapter focuses on six resourcing issues that should be considered: dedicated funds and funding sources, time, specialised in-house expertise, staff with competencies, a broad knowledge base and relevant relationships.

Programme shape

Funds and funding sources

Most organisations and staff involved in civil society development identify lack of funds as the most inhibiting factor to the organisation's or programme's development. Donor trends over the last decade have increasingly been to mainstream funding of civil society capacity building within broader sector programme funding. An additional current trend is to channel civil society support funds via bilateral support programmes which are managed by national governments. It is becoming increasingly difficult to access official donor funding geared towards direct support for the development of CSOs which does not have conditions set in terms of predefined goals and targets, often expressed in relation to agreed global or national strategies.

Part Two, Chapter 7

It may seem that in a scarce funding climate, being selective about funding is a luxury that cannot be afforded. However, taking money from sources that are not supportive of the programme approach, or that are operating with agendas which may run counter to the overall motivation behind the work will constrain the programme and is likely to be more detrimental in the long term.

> **Critical thoughts**
>
> Back donors have their own agenda. Are you clear about any potential donor's core interests in funding civil society capacity building work, over and above any stated goals or purpose of the relevant funding scheme?
>
> What is the degree of shared interests and potential conflicting interests and are there opportunities to discuss them?

It is important to be aware of the potential range of funding sources available for capacity building work, including less well known trust funds, foundations etc. In a recent INGO survey 40% of respondents estimated that almost one third of their overall programme funds were spent on capacity building work. The table below shows the range of sources of funding for the capacity building work of the INGO respondents:

Funding source	Percentage of INGOs
INGOs own unrestricted funds	72%
Own government civil society units	54%
Own government bilateral programmes	54%
Foundations	51%
EU funding from Brussels	41%
Other	38%
EU decentralised funds	24%
Own regional/local government	12%
UNDP	15%
Other UN body	15%
Regional Development Bank/World Bank	16%

Source: Lipson, B and Warren, H. 'Taking stock'. INTRAC, 2006.

Specialised in-house expertise

Each organisation engaging in capacity building work needs to reflect on the degree to which it wishes to invest in specialised in-house capacity building expertise. This can be in the form of individual staff members whose job is to provide that expertise or it could be one area of responsibility within a more generic programme or policy adviser post. The INGO survey indicated a high level of commitment to investing in such expertise, which can be seen as a tangible indication to partners and donors of a commitment to the organisation's own capacity building. The following are some examples of the options available at organisation-level posts:

Cross Organisational Methods or 'Quality' Specialist

Responsible for cross-cutting themes such as learning, systems and methodologies, knowledge management, impact assessment and mainstreaming of capacity building. They will be concerned with their own organisation's capacity building as well as having an overview of capacity building programmes. They may not be specialised in capacity building.

Organisational Capacity Building Specialist

Responsible for organisation-wide capacity building thematic issues, for example capacity building framework or policy development. They will have an overview of capacity building programmes within the organisation, whether they are generic or specific. They may be involved in programme design, monitoring issues of consistency, policy implementation, cross programmatic learning, monitoring and evaluation etc. They are likely to have an in-depth knowledge and experience of capacity building at all levels, and be familiar with the literature and the organisations specialising in capacity building.

> **Case example**
>
> Organisation X is an international organisation with member organisations at national and regional levels. A recent organisational review indicated there was not a coherent approach to the support provided to these member organisations, as well as a serious lack of learning on this work. As well as being financially costly to the organisation, it also began to impact on policy issues, resulting in a breakdown of trust between the membership. It was recommended that an organisational capacity building specialist be recruited to assist in building a common framework and approach to the growth and support to the organisation as a whole.

Capacity Building Programme Specialist

Responsible for a specific capacity building programme. They may be based at head office with regional advisors or regionally or country based. They are most likely to have had direct capacity building experience, as well as an understanding of organisation development and civil society development issues.

> **Critical thoughts**
>
> Do you and your organisation have the appropriate expertise to carry out capacity building work?
>
> Have you gained credibility in the eyes of your partners and donors by demonstrating your commitment to increasing your own capacity building knowledge, skills and expertise?
>
> Have you identified gaps in expertise? What action can you take?

Broad knowledge base

It is also important to consider investing in building up a broad knowledge base around capacity building. This can be done in different ways:

1. Investing in a resource centre
2. Investing in staff attending training, workshops and conferences on capacity building
3. Establishing an internal community of diverse staff who focus on building and sharing knowledge
4. Setting up an intranet discussion site
5. Encouraging debate on other specialist capacity building websites

6. Investing in knowledge management systems, so that information is shared effectively
7. Setting up a capacity building newsletter with inter-regional contributions.

The following example illustrates the activities undertaken by an international organisation to address the issue of increasing its knowledge base.

> **Case example**
>
> Organisation A is developing a function focused on facilitating learning across the institute and building a knowledge base, which is working to provide:
>
> - conceptual and methodological information to be used for building capacity for constituency building and resource mobilisation.
> - a selection of tools which can be contextualised.
> - a selection of brief, accessible case studies (from the institution and other organisations) which illustrate successful and less successful initiatives to mobilise people and funds. In addition, production of other dissemination materials to be included in a variety of institution-wide publications.
> - a database of local providers of training and capacity building services, organised by region.
> - a resource library of literature on relevant mobilisation subjects (civil society strengthening; capacity building; organisation development; governance issues; leadership; relationship building; monitoring and evaluation; advocacy; resource mobilisation; membership recruitment/retention strategies etc).
> - analysis of major issues, emerging trends and growth patterns of key social movements and civil society sectors across the world.
> - facilitation of cross-institution capacity building, prioritising initiatives within the regions but also identifying opportunities for cross-regional work. Facilitation of exchange of experiences; 'institutional apprenticeships' etc.
> - together with other colleagues, develop methods for monitoring and evaluation of capacity building.
> - translation of key materials into other languages.

Part Two, Chapter 5

Staff competencies

Having focused on the organisational resources, it is also important to focus on the appropriate range of required staff competencies and the range of roles that staff will undertake in relation to capacity building work. Competencies relate to skills, knowledge, attitudes, behaviour and experience of an individual and are one of the critical resources in any programming work. The values and principles of an individual also have a significant impact on the work that is carried out and means of checking out these more intangible areas will be important. Part Two explores values and principles in detail.

→ Part Two, Chapter 6

Competencies for a capacity building specialist will include both soft and hard skills. Soft skills are associated with processes and people and include, for example, facilitation skills, negotiating skills, adaptive skills and training skills. Hard skills are related to systems and tasks and focus on more tangible elements of a job, for example, achieving the objectives, reporting and budgeting. Specific for a capacity building provider will be skills related to contracting, negotiating, using participatory methods, and an understanding of working with local consultants and local capacity building providers. Other more generic characteristics of individuals working in a development context include: an openness to listen and to learn, the ability to establish and nurture relationships, understanding of process and task issues, humility, self-awareness and the ability for action and reflection. Part Two includes a self-assessment tool to assist the reader in reflecting on some of the personal qualities of the capacity building provider.

> **? Critical thoughts**
>
> Do you and/or your organisation have the competencies for capacity building work?
>
> Where are the competency gaps? Are there sufficient resources to fill the gaps and is it easy to access skilled and competent staff?

Relevant relationships

Relationships are a key resource for capacity building work. If capacity building is to be sustainable and have the impact it seeks, then relationships become the cornerstone for capacity building work at all levels. It may be useful to identify external reference points in relation to capacity building debates, technical advice, sharing and learning, etc. Building up a database of such contacts could be critical to ensuring that everyone in the organisation has access to data on who they might be able to approach for what kind of support, information and advice.

→ Part Two, Chapter 2

> **? Critical thoughts**
>
> Do you network with other capacity building sponsors and providers?
>
> Do you share knowledge, advice and learning? Have you joined concrete initiatives such as topic-led learning communities on different capacity building issues?

SUMMARY

This chapter focuses on six areas of resourcing to consider early on: dedicated funds and funding sources, time, specialised in-house expertise, staff with competencies, a broad knowledge base and relevant relationships.

Key points include:

- Funding sources that are not supportive of the programme approach, or that are operating with agendas which may run counter to the agenda which shaped the programme, will constrain the work and are likely to be detrimental to the programme in the long term. Identify the degree of shared interests and potential conflicting interests.
- Identify the appropriate expertise to carry out capacity building work for you and the organisation – consider investing in building up a broad knowledge base in the area of capacity building.
- Be aware of the range of staff competencies required and the range of roles that staff will undertake in relation to capacity building work. The values and principles of an individual also have a significant impact on the work that is carried out.
- Identify external reference points in relation to capacity building knowledge debates, technical advice, sharing and learning, etc.

RECOMMENDED READING

See General Reading section for references to websites for learning communities, resources on capacity building etc.

Chapter 8
Monitoring and evaluating

Monitoring and evaluating capacity building programmes is undertaken for two reasons – one focused on being able to account for the investment made, and the other focused on having information in order to learn from what works and what doesn't work. Accountability is a necessary aspect of development practice but unfortunately tends to dominate general debates on both capacity building, and monitoring and evaluation. Particularly widespread is the upward accountability drive (to donors) when often the need to be accountable to the participants of capacity building programmes is overlooked. Capacity building programming should attempt to change minds to an attitude of accountability *and learning* simultaneously. The action–reflection cycle emphasised throughout this guide reinforces this.

Programme shape

When it comes to impact assessment there are even more challenges. It is notoriously difficult to measure the impact of capacity building, which is a critical issue when designing and implementing a capacity building programme. All too often, investments in organisational capacity take time to impact on the quality of work or the services offered, and efforts to link investment in new capacity with higher quality of life are fraught with methodological difficulties.

This chapter explores monitoring, evaluation and impact assessment, looking at the challenges that surround assessment of capacity building programmes and means of overcoming these. Different levels and types of indicators are illustrated through examples.

Learning

This chapter briefly introduces the topic of learning to enable the reader to consider learning as a lens through which to view monitoring, evaluation and accountability. It is also to emphasise the importance of learning in the design and implementation of a capacity building programme. Learning is considered in relation to change and organisational values and principles at greater length in Part Two.

....
 Part Two, Chapter 5
....

Learning implies having an approach that enables all stakeholders to constantly reflect and change, with an emphasis on a continuous process of action–reflection, rather than at set points in time. Therefore it is legitimised as an important element of a capacity building programme, and becomes a way of thinking and part of the programme's cultural dynamic.

> Part One, Chapter 4, learning cycle

Benefits of learning include increasing effectiveness, developing capacity, facilitating the best use of limited resources, helping to strengthen development relationships and partnerships and closing the gap between planning, monitoring and evaluation.

If the motivation, the means and opportunity for learning has been created, then an environment is in place to enable a learning approach to the monitoring and evaluation of the capacity building programme. Care must be taken however, to ensure that learning is not subsumed into the monitoring and evaluation paradigm, whereby learning mechanisms are in place but the results are used for evaluative purposes rather than developmental. Learning is not a function of accountability and should not be reduced to merely providing additional information for monitoring and evaluation. The remaining sections consider monitoring, evaluation and impact assessment in the context of a **learning culture**.

Indicators

Indicators are observable changes or events which provide evidence that something has happened, whether an output is delivered, or an immediate or long-term effect has occurred. Indicators lie at the heart of a monitoring and evaluation system, and their identification must be integral to the design process. Indicators will relate to the (qualitative or quantitative) measurement of different aspects.

Capacity indicators

These are the core reference point for any capacity building programme, and they have been explored in depth in Part One. A capacity indicator describes a specific capacity area. It should be appropriate to the specific characteristics of the organisation and the environment in which it operates. For example the type of the organisation if it is an organisational capacity indicator, or the cultural context if it is a sector-wide capacity indicator.

> Part One, Chapters 2 and 3

Capacity indicators can be used in two different but inter-related ways:

- as descriptions of the **current state**, for example as used in organisational or capacity assessment exercises
- as descriptions of the **desired future state**, for example when used to illustrate the specific objectives of capacity building activities.

The second of these is of particular relevance to monitoring and evaluation as the capacity indicator is used to describe the desired **outcome** of any capacity building intervention.

Case example

PROTECT is an INGO which is implementing a global HIV/AIDS awareness programme in collaboration with a network of local partners. To complement the programme, they decided to invest in developing partner capacity through a focused Strategic Partner Capacity Building Programme. The ultimate aim of the programme is to increase HIV/AIDS awareness in newly affected countries. The goal is to strengthen the capacity of local partners to deliver awareness programmes. The initial scoping and design work established three programme objectives:

1. partners have the capacity to design and implement effective awareness raising programmes
2. partners have the capacity to learn from the programmes they implement and introduce changes accordingly
3. partners have a strong network of allies, collaborators and peers who are working in the field of HIV/AIDS awareness.

After the initial scoping and pre-design work, a more detailed phase of capacity assessments took place. PROTECT staff, together with a task group of partners, worked with a capacity building specialist to design an assessment method and tools. As part of this process, they identified the key capacity areas that would be the focus of the capacity building programme. These included, amongst others:

- **To be:** Organisational capacity for learning (culture, leadership)
  Human resources capacity – distribution of roles/responsibilities to reflect the new work
- **To do:** Communications and media skills
  Understanding of awareness-raising strategies
  Programme management competencies
  Monitoring and evaluation capacity, particularly as applied to M&E of public awareness work
- **To relate:** Strategic management of relationships

For each capacity area, a benchmark capacity indicator was established. This described the ideal characteristics of that capacity, in relation to what was known to be required to achieve the three programme objectives. These became the generic capacity indicators which would serve as the reference point for the capacity assessments, and also would be the target for capacity building initiatives. The indicators were relatively complex, with different elements within them. For example, the capacity indicator established for the strategic management of relationships was:

> 'The organisation has the skills to map out a full range of actors engaged in HIV/AIDS awareness work in their country, and in the region in which they are based.'

Managers are able to make clear choices about which of these actors are most relevant for the organisation, based on their understanding of the organisation's values, mission and strategic direction.

> Staff have the skills and attitudes appropriate for effective dialogue and negotiation with the identified actors. The organisation has developed written formal memorandum of agreements which are used effectively when collaborative initiatives are undertaken.
>
> The organisation has sufficient communications infrastructure to be able to maintain effective communication with the actors. The organisation has in place, and is successfully using, an easily accessible contacts database.
>
> The organisation actively seeks out feedback from its contacts, on all aspects of the relationship.
>
> PROTECT is clear that the approach to these generic indicators needs to be flexible, with sensitivity to cultural and general environmental factors being a key element. The partners have access to a Capacity Building Fund, and they use those resources to identify and work with local capacity building consultants in the application of the assessment method and tools. A capacity building plan is developed as an output of that process, which forms the basis for the activities to be carried out. Where similar activities are identified, PROTECT encourages partners to pool their resources wherever feasible.

In this example there are a number of indicators that will serve as reference points for assessing changes obtained during the programme. The initial capacity assessments provide a baseline of the current state of each capacity at the start of the programme – with the local capacity building consultants facilitating a process of establishing the degree of fit with the description provided in each indicator. The partners continuously monitor progress and measure their successes in terms of reaching a close match with the indicator.

The organisational capacity indicators will provide information about the changes achieved at the level of individual organisations. It may be that the programme is working at other levels – networks, sub-sector, civil society sector as a whole. The principle is the same as described above. It is necessary to work with capacity indicators or descriptions of the desired state of each capacity area in relation with the objectives of the capacity building initiative.

Programme indicators

The measurement of capacity indicators will also provide data on which overall programme progress towards its objectives can be assessed. However, it is probable that these would need to be supplemented by other types of indicators which might be pitched more at the level of the programme's goal and ultimate aim. This is entering the more familiar programming logic, whereby different levels of change are identified and indicators developed to describe them.

The indicators for the achievement of the programme goal and aim in the case above would include areas such as:

- increased coverage achieved by partners' awareness-raising efforts
- increased reference to the partners' viewpoints in the media, general public etc

- increased knowledge about HIV/AIDS amongst target population.

The many issues about measuring change at these levels will be explored later in this chapter (see page 167).

Process indicators

These are indicators related to the process of capacity building itself, for example degree to which the process used was in itself empowering, inclusive etc. Unfortunately often very little attention is paid to this area in the design and implementation of capacity building programmes.

It is important to jointly identify these indicators with key stakeholders at the design phase. The sponsors, donors, participating CSOs etc will all have views on what will make a successful capacity building process. The identification of process indicators can be achieved through discussions about the range of capacity building methods and facilitation styles and their appropriateness to the objectives and context of the programme.

The values of the capacity building specialists in the programme will influence the process indicators. The dialogue should be participatory and inclusive , allowing for a range of opinions while aiming for consensus on the indicators.

↔ Part Two, Chapter 6

In addition, the sponsor of the capacity building programme may have a number of policies or a statement of principles regarding their views on good capacity building practice. These will be a key source for identifying process indicators as it is through these indicators that good practice principles are best measured.

↔ Part Two, Chapter 4

Monitoring and evaluation

Monitoring is the systematic and continuous assessment of progress of a piece of work over time, which checks that things are going to plan and enables positive adjustments to be made. **Evaluation** is the periodic assessment of the relevance, performance, efficiency and impact of a piece of work with respect to its related objectives. An evaluation is usually carried out at some significant stage in the development of a piece of work for example at the end of a planning period, the move into a new phase, or in response to a particular critical issue.

There is often a perceived gap between generating information through monitoring and evaluation and using this for future planning. What this gap represents is often the **absence of mechanisms for learning** in the design of monitoring and evaluation systems. If the factors facilitating a learning environment are actively present as explored above, then the gap between monitoring, evaluation and planning should be reduced, as information and knowledge from monitoring and evaluating will be used for the purposes of *learning (for future planning)* and *accountability*.

> Part Two, Chapter 5 and Part Three, Chapter 3

The way the capacity building programme will be monitored and evaluated must be considered at the design and planning stage.

Key considerations include:

- If changes (impact) are to be observed, it will be important to record the situation *before* the programme starts.
- For monitoring to be incorporated into the management of the programme, the appropriate systems must be set up from the beginning.
- If the programme's progress towards outputs, outcomes and impact is to be monitored and evaluated, these must be clearly defined.
- Types and levels of indicators must be considered, for example, individual to societal level and outcome and process type capacity indicators.
- In order to develop a participatory monitoring and evaluation system which includes primary stakeholders, they must be involved in deciding what changes should be monitored.

General challenges to monitoring and evaluating capacity building work are most often concerned with unclear programme design; measuring complex, intangible and qualitative change; demonstrating causality and attribution; responding to context and culture and too great an emphasis on accountability to donors, thus reducing the process to results against investment costs.

> **? Critical thoughts**
>
> Who have you designed the monitoring and evaluation system for?
>
> If it is to meet donor requirements of tangible and measurable outputs and outcomes, and how would this fit with a capacity building programme that is most likely going to be working with qualitative and intangible change processes?

Monitoring

Monitoring must be seen as a tool to be used by all stakeholders, not just management or evaluators. The monitoring system should be defined in a participatory way at the design phase of the programme, not at the implementation phase. The following questions should be discussed:

1. What information should be used?
2. Who will collect the information?
3. How will monitoring information be collected?
4. When will information be collected?
5. Who will organise and analyse monitoring information?
6. How will findings from monitoring be used?

In answering these questions, consider ways and methods that are not only about checking on progress, but also ensuring participation and incorporating a shared learning approach into the overall programme dynamic. Some examples include:

- relevant stakeholders keep regular learning journals, shared at periodic progress meetings
- opportunities are created for client feedback on periodic consultant visits
- user or advisory groups meet which regularly reflect on progress and feed into reporting flow.

In addition, the design phase needs to consider how to track capacity building processes and how they are changing people's lives at all levels. This may include the relationships within the programme, the power dynamics, the values underpinning the programme, participation etc.

Examples include:

Peer monitoring of staff meetings to observe how newly acquired facilitation skills are being put into practice to encourage more participation and less hierarchical decision making. At the same time, observations may also take place of the power relations between staff and managers, the informal and formal power dynamics at play and the culture of the organisation as expressed through the meetings they have. Structured feedback could be offered at the end of each meeting as part of the capacity building process.

Self monitoring of newly elected chairwomen of local women's CBOs, in relation to effectiveness in meetings, ability to make decisions, use of facilitation skills, ensuring all members' voices are heard etc. The self monitoring process becomes both a monitoring tool and a capacity building process.

Evaluation

Having ensured a participatory monitoring process that enables learning to take place at all programme levels, the rationale and understanding of evaluation also needs to be made explicit at the design phase. A key question will be 'accountability to whom?'. Most often the answer will be primarily the donors, but, more especially in a capacity building programme, an additional question will be, 'how are the clients incorporated in the evaluation process?'. This might involve the organisation negotiating directly with consultants on the terms of reference, selection of the evaluation team, methodologies to be used, stakeholders to be consulted with etc. Checks and balances can be put in place through the negotiation process with stakeholders, consultants and donors.

Engaging in evaluation processes raises the question of what is being evaluated. Most often evaluation is concerned with the inputs, outputs and outcomes against the original objectives of the programme, i.e. what was planned. However, especially within capacity building programmes, with intangible and often complex and qualitative processes, another question to ask is 'what has emerged?'.

Part Three, Chapter 2

If a learning culture is at the heart of the programme, then flexibility within the programme design to respond to unplanned opportunities and outcomes will have already been established. For example, what has emerged may be more positive or negative than what was planned. Either way, the programme design needs to account for this flexibility in relation to the pre-defined objectives and feel comfortable and confident that what has emerged, rather than what was planned, is often the nature of capacity building programming.

Part Three, Chapter 4

Case example

A leadership development programme for board members and senior management of NGOs was established, sponsored by a multilateral development agency. The aim was to strengthen the NGO sub-sector by investing in a peer group of key leaders. However, as the two-year programme progressed the participants were headhunted by international NGOs who were looking for local staff to replace the expatriate managers of their country programmes. In response the design of the programme changed. More participants were trained and a new junior management coaching and training programme introduced to complement the main programme and ensure succession planning for the future leadership.

Often, evaluations are set points in time when the power dynamics are temporarily reversed as external evaluators come to interact with the capacity building programme. It is important that in designing the evaluation, due care and attention is paid to the values and principles of the programme itself. For example, if participation is a core value of the programme, then how can this value be expressed in the design of the evaluation? Suggestions include:

- external evaluators being accompanied by members of stakeholder groups (for example CSO staff members, or community based volunteers) as an observation and learning process
- multi-stakeholder/disciplinary groups, including external and internal evaluators
- primary stakeholders designing the evaluation process together with external evaluators
- using participatory, verbal and visual evaluation tools (for example story telling, drama, before/during/after mapping, workshops).

In addition, if gender equality is a programme value, then the make-up of the evaluation team must reflect this. Likewise the evaluation plan must enable both men and women to participate equally in the process, such as accessible venues, timings etc.

> 'There is also the view that to capture the changes that are of most importance to developmental practitioners we cannot reduce things of quality to quantities and little boxes. We end up considering only that part of what is important that is easily measured.'
> (Taylor 2003)

Impact

Impact concerns long-term and sustainable changes in the lives of stakeholders, linked to a given intervention. One image that is used is to liken impact with a pebble that lands in a pond. When the pebble lands in the water, a series of ripples flow outwards from the point of entry across the surface of the pond. Thus, ripples may flow outwards from changes brought about at an individual level to the organisational and societal levels. For example, a training course may lead to improved knowledge as well as new skills and attitudes at an individual level. That individual applies these within their work, which leads to organisational changes. The changes improve the performance of the organisation, which benefits those people who the organisation works for.

In some cases there may not be such a linear, causal relationship at play. For example, it is possible to see changes in individuals' behaviour when new organisational systems or procedures are introduced, and both the organisational and the individual changes reinforce each other and contribute to improved performance i.e. there are several 'waves' operating simultaneously.

Impact can be related either to the specific goals of an intervention or to unanticipated change caused by an intervention. Such unanticipated changes may also occur in the lives of people who were not expected to be affected by the intervention. Impact can be either positive or negative.

The focus of many monitoring and evaluation systems is the measurement of outputs and outcomes (related to activities and objectives of the programme respectively). Assessing impact is more complex. It is not represented by numerical indicators which allow for simple measurement, but must usually be described as a qualitative change, over a longer period of time. Impact assessment is primarily concerned with observable changes or events, which can either be directly or indirectly attributed to the programme interventions, both positively or negatively. The impact assessment seeks to provide evidence that change has happened.

Part Three, Chapters 3 and 4

The link between impact and capacity building becomes more obvious, as both involve long-term qualitative change, the emphasis being not only on the programme outcomes but change in people's lives. For example, a capacity building programme aimed at helping an intermediary HIV/AIDS NGO towards independence will want to know that in so doing, people living with HIV/AIDS (for whom the organisation exists) will benefit in the long term.

In designing a capacity building programme, it is important to be clear about the extent of the desired impact of the programme. Change may occur at multiple levels (for example individual, organisational, sectoral and societal). The programme needs to be clear about what level of impact will be assessed, which will be linked to the programme goal and objectives. If, for example, the programme has a long-term goal linked to poverty reduction, the challenge for assessing impact will lie in making the ultimate connection between the programme and positive change in poor people's lives.

→ Part Two, Chapter 5

There are a number of approaches and methods that can be used to assess impact as well as some issues to consider when designing and implementing the programme:

- **Baseline data**

If possible, it is important to generate sufficient baseline data on which to measure the quality and depth of any changes that may occur (both intentional and unintentional). Evaluations will measure moments in time of the intervention against the baseline data, impact assessment will measure longer term outcomes, after the programme has finished. If a good monitoring system is in place prior to the implementation phase then baseline data will be more readily accessed.

→ Part Three, Chapter 2

> **Critical thoughts**
>
> What baseline data does the programme need and how might you gather it?
>
> Who will be involved and what will be the purpose?
>
> Have you considered the possible unintended outcomes or negative effects of the programme?

- **Plausible association**

Any particular capacity building intervention is merely one intervention among many that bring about change. Organisational and environmental changes, initiatives at community level, or development interventions by other agencies in the same area are bound to affect the changes induced by a particular capacity building intervention. But by using the concept of plausible association, it is possible to judge whether change at one level does indeed ripple out to bring about changes at a wider level. This, in turn, depends on the baseline data available for assessments of the quality and significance of the changes which have taken place. Consequently, collecting and analysing such data can help understand the dynamics of change. By applying concepts such as plausible association, these processes may help demonstrate the link between a particular capacity building intervention and its wider developmental benefits.

MONITORING AND EVALUATING

> **Critical thoughts**
>
> Are you attempting to directly attribute all elements of the capacity building programme to specified outcomes and impact? Is this realistic and feasible?
>
> By applying the concept of plausible association, and ensuring that sufficient baseline data is available, can you more realistically make links between certain capacity building interventions and change that has taken place, using the ripple effect?

- **Most Significant Change**

As a story-based technique the 'Most Significant Change' (MSC) approach can help to identify and give value to changes that were unintended or unexpected but were nevertheless significant impacts for those involved. Experience suggests that the advantages of using MSC are its ability to capture and consolidate the different perspectives of stakeholders, to aid understanding and conceptualisation of complex change, and to enhance organisational learning. The potential constraints of using MSC as an approach to evaluating capacity building lie in meeting the needs of externally driven evaluation processes and dealing with subjectivity and bias. The case example below illustrates the use of MSC in a capacity building programme evaluation.

> **Case example**
>
> Participants in the evaluation process felt that using a story-based approach was very useful in helping CABUNGO to understand the impact it is having on the organisational capacity of its clients, and how its services could be improved. In particular, it yielded information that might have been missed through a conventional use of performance indicators. CABUNGO used a holistic OD process that resulted in a wide range of complex and often intangible internal and external impacts that are very difficult to predict in advance. An open and unstructured interview process allowed the flexibility for interviewees to express the changes that they perceived as most significant.
>
> The key advantages of using MSC were:
>
> - **Capturing and consolidating different perspectives** from a wide range of stakeholders about the significance of the change that had been achieved. By not focusing on predetermined outcomes, the process helped to identify unexpected change, such as improvements in the relationships between CBOs and their communities.
>
> - **Understanding and conceptualising complex change.** A clearer, richer understanding of the change that had resulted from CABUNGO's capacity building interventions was identified. The process of discussing and analysing the stories collected provided an opportunity to assess and conceptualise the particular characteristics of organisational capacity building – the systemic, multidimensional and dynamic nature of organisational change processes.
>
> - **Enhancing organisational learning.** The purpose of the evaluation was 'to enhance CABUNGO's learning and therefore improve our performance'. Using the MSC approach provided an effective opportunity for CABUNGO staff to:

collect stories of experiences; analyse and reflect on these; use this analysis to conceptualise the impact that had been achieved; discuss and define areas to improve the quality of their practice and integrate these findings into their strategic planning processes. Consequently, a powerful advantage of using MSC is the way it can make a significant contribution to organisational learning.

The potential constraints of using the MSC approach to evaluate capacity building were identified as follows:

• **Meeting the needs of externally driven evaluation processes.** As a self-evaluation process that was internally driven, using MSC proved to be a valuable learning process for CABUNGO as it identified unexpected change. However, what is less clear is whether the findings would meet the needs of an evaluation that is externally driven, for instance, one that demands specific quantitative data according to donor requirements. This could be overcome by combining MSC with other, more quantitative evaluation methodologies.

• **Dealing with subjectivity and bias.** MSC is based on the perceptions of change of those interviewed and the opinions of the people involved in the selection process. This can lead to criticisms of subjectivity and bias. This may be less of a potential constraint where the evaluation findings are being used for learning purposes rather than as an accountability mechanism to donors.

Revising the MSC approach

CABUNGO felt that the MSC approach could become a useful part of their M&E system which could relatively easily be integrated as a more routine part of the organisation's way of working. This could include:

1. OD practitioners spontaneously writing down the stories they hear during the normal course of their work.

2. Interviewing stakeholders, such as staff of client organisations, board members, community members etc, or holding group discussions as part of the follow up provided after capacity building interventions.

3. Asking clients to document their own stories. This would require providing enough information to ensure that they know what is expected of them.

4. Holding periodic evaluation summits to review the stories that have been collected, select the most significant ones and feed these into annual and strategic planning processes.

Source: adapted from Wiggley, R. *Learning from Capacity Building Practice*, INTRAC, 2006

SUMMARY

This chapter highlights the following:

- the importance of a learning culture that becomes a 'way of life' in any capacity building programme
- the challenges of monitoring and evaluating capacity building programmes and ways of overcoming them
- the need to change a mindset from one of measurable and tangible results to one of flexibility, adaptability, and uncertainty
- using methodologies such as the concept of plausible association, baseline data and innovative participatory methods to assess the impact of capacity building programmes more effectively.

RECOMMENDED READING

Bakewell, O. *Sharpening the Development Process: A Practical Guide to Monitoring and Evaluation*. INTRAC, 2003

Davies, R and Dart, J. *The Most Significant Change (MSC) Technique: A Guide to its Use.* 2005, available at www.mande.co.uk

Hailey, J, James, R and Wrigley, R. *Rising to the Challenges: Assessing the Impacts of Organisational Capacity Building*. INTRAC, 2005

James, R. 'The ripple model', cited in *People and Change: Exploring Capacity Building in NGOs*. INTRAC, 2002

James, R. *Practical Guidelines for the Monitoring and Evaluation of Capacity Building.* INTRAC, 2002

Pratt, B. 'The Monitoring and Evaluation of Civil Society Support Programmes', in *Changing Expectations? The Theory and Practice of Civil Society in International Development*. INTRAC, 2003

Final thoughts

'Values come into all areas of thinking and behaviour. Values are what we consider important, but we may not be consciously aware of them.'
(De Bono, E. *The Six Value Medals*, 2005)

We, the authors, agree with De Bono when he writes about how, at the human level, values direct and change our perceptions, affect our decision making and are the 'underlying drivers that bring about our emotions'. In essence, our capacity building practice is influenced by the values we carry as individuals, and as organisations. Yet so often this is not explicitly recognised. This book aims to provide a practical approach to working with explicitly **values-based** capacity building programmes.

Our approach to writing this book

As authors, we of course have our own values or set of ideas and qualities that are informed by, and in turn inform, our beliefs, principles and aspirations. In writing this practical guide we have placed an emphasis on sharing our ideas and experiences of shaping capacity building programmes without stating overtly our own personal values.

We recognise that readers will be operating from within very diverse societal and organisational contexts, which together with their own personal worldviews means that their interpretation of the content will be equally diverse. Our aim has been to respect this diversity and provide some prompts for thinking – not to provide the answers to the questions.

That said, the overall impression may be that this publication fits within the predominant technocratic approach to capacity building. We would rather see this publication as a bridge – something which links the need to have robust capacity building practice with the equally important need to ensure that we do not lose our values along the journey towards such robustness. We seek a robust capacity building practice grounded in strong and **clearly articulated** values.

The idea for this book came in response to a perceived gap. It appeared that there was little explicit literature focused on the practicalities of designing capacity building programmes which link with the values held important by the organisation. Generally there would seem to be few internal organisational procedures, systems and tools which help staff systematically check the coherence between the design of a programme seeking concrete capacity building results and the values of the organisation, as expressed both in those results but also in the *methods* or *processes* employed.

Why is a values-based framework important?

We hope that this framework goes some way in addressing this gap. Finding a meeting point between values and practice is one of the crucial issues faced by practitioners who are committed to a developmental and transformational capacity building practice.

However, we recognise that there exist many contradictions and constraints. Many core values relating to participation, empowerment, demand-led processes and so on may be clearly articulated in the design process, but not clearly in evidence once the programme is underway. We need to analyse what is holding us back, and decide whether we wish to act to address these constraints. There is a good synthesis of these issues in Chapter 7 of the sister publication, *Capacity Building For NGOs: Making It Work* and we do not wish to cover the same ground here.

We believe there are like-minded individuals and organisations who are searching for alternatives to the technocratic approach, and there is scope for a joint construction of those alternatives. We could share our ideas and experiences of developing new discourses, analytical and methodological frameworks and behaviours which explicitly articulate our values. We could be held accountable to each other for our implementation of these, and could, just possibly, jointly establish a new paradigm for capacity building – an ethical paradigm.

General reading

Books and papers

Baser, H and Morgan, P et al. *Capacity, Change and Performance – a study report*. ECDPM, 2008

Eade, D. *Capacity Building: An Approach to People Centred Development*. Oxfam, 1997

Fowler, A. *Striking a Balance: A Guide to Enhancing the Effectiveness of Non-Governmental Organisations in International Development*. Earthscan/INTRAC, 1997

Fowler, A. *The Virtuous Spiral: A Guide to Sustainability for NGOs in International Development*. Earthscan/INTRAC, 2000

Fowler, A. *Systemic Change for Promoting Local Capacity Development*. Paper for workshop discussion, 2006

James, R. *Demystifying Organisation Development: Practical Capacity Building Experiences of African NGOs*. INTRAC, 1998

James, R. *Power and Partnership: Experiences of NGO Capacity-Building*. INTRAC, 2001

James, R and Hailey, J. *Capacity Building for NGOs: Making It Work*. INTRAC, 2007

Lipson, B & Warren, H, (2006) 'Taking Stock: a snapshot of INGO engagement in civil society capacity building'. Civil Society and Capacity Building Conference Paper, INTRAC

OECD-DAC Network on Governance. *The Challenge of Capacity Development: Working towards good practice*. 2006

OECD-DAC. *Capacity Development: Accra and beyond – summary workshop conclusions*. 2008, available at: www.oecd.org/dac/governance/capacitydevelopment

Paton, R and McCalman, J. *Change Management: A Guide to Effective Implementation*. Sage, 2000

Van Rooy, A. *Civil Society and the Aid Industry*. Earthscan, 1998

Wheatley, M. *Finding Our Way: Leadership for an Uncertain Time*. Berrett-Koehler, 2007

Useful websites

www.acdi-cida.gc.ca – Canadian donor agency website, with a collection of interesting materials on capacity development.

www.capacity.org – specialist website dedicated to capacity building. Strong orientation towards public sector and official donor agencies.

www.capacity.undp.org – website of UNDP with range of materials, links, tools etc.

www.cdra.org.za – website of South African civil society support organisation, specialised in organisational capacity building.

www.civicus.org/resources – practical tools available for download on this website of the global civil society network, Civicus.

www.impactalliance.org – website of global multi-actor network initiated by PACT. Very useful materials.

www.intrac.org – website covering many aspects of civil society strengthening. Includes the specialised Praxis pages which contain reflection papers produced by capacity building practitioners.

www.mande.org – independent website dedicated to the subject of monitoring and evaluation and impact assessment.

www.ngomanager.org – World Bank supported website with some practical materials.

www.pria.org – website of Indian civil society support organisation, with useful practical manuals available for purchase.

www.proteusinitiative.org – specialist website based on a specific approach (Goethiesm) to organisational development and change. Founded by Allan Kaplan.

www.pso.nl – Dutch support organisation with strong emphasis on learning and knowledge management.

www.worldbank.org/capacity – The World Bank Institute's Capacity Development Resource Center. Primarily official agency and national/local government-orientated materials.

Appendix
Capacity building programming – Framework guide

Use this guide to systematically analyse the responses to a series of prompt questions, related to the overall programming framework presented in this book.

Core areas analysis		
Core area	**Questions**	**Your response**
1. Agenda: How clear is your 'head'?	• Why is your organisation interested in civil society capacity building? How does this relate to its vision of the role that CSOs play in social change and development? • What is your answer to the 'capacity building for what?' question? • Where would you see your position regarding the 'functional' or 'intrinsic' approach to this work? • How explicit are you about the agenda?	
2. Concepts, methods, tools: How strong are your 'arms'?	**a. Conceptual clarity** • Do you have agreed understandings on what you mean by 'capacity' and 'capacity building'? • Are there shared models of civil society; organisations; capacity change and development? • Would a capacity building policy or other written reference help? • How engaged are you in the broader debates about capacity building and specifically about 'good practice'? **b. Methods, tools** • Do you draw on a broad range of approaches and methods in designing your work? • Have you a wide range of tools or capacity building activities upon which to draw and adapt according to specific contexts and circumstances? • How do you approach the contextualisation of your work?	

3. Programming choices: **How firm are your 'legs'?**	**a. Programme definition** • Are you looking at a 'stand-alone' dedicated capacity building programme, cross-cutting or 'mainstreaming'? • How are you ensuring the 'programmatic' in this work? **b. Goal/objectives:** • Have you undertaken sufficient mapping or diagnostic work in order to define realistic capacity building goal/objectives? **c. Levels/approach** • What level/s will you work at? Individual, community, organisation, sub-sector (networks), sector (civil society as a whole)…? **d Targets** • Which types of organisation are you considering to be participants in your capacity building work? **e. Types of intervention** • What range of capacity building activities will you be drawing on? • Do you have the appropriate mix for the type of participating CSOs; for the context; for the objectives of the programme? Are they reinforcing each other? **f. Role** • What roles does your organisation adopt? (funder, information provider, advocate, faciliatator) • Are your staff actively engaged in delivering capacity building activities? What are the implications of this?	

4. Coherence and linkages	**a. Linkages within your organisation** • What formal or non-formal linkages exist between your capacity building work and your organisation's other programmes? Livelihoods, peace building, emergency relief…? **b. Geographical coherence and linkages** • What coherence and linkages are evidenced at global, regional and country levels in respect of capacity building programming? **d. Managing context** • What are the policies, procedures or mechanisms for ensuring programme coherence across varied contexts or for negotiating diversity? **e. Mainstreamed gender/HIV/AIDS issues** • How are these, and any other mainstreamed issues, being addressed in your capacity building work?	
5. Relationships	**a. Partnership** • How does it express itself in the capacity building work? **b. Range of relationships** • What is the diversity and quality of relations in the capacity building work? With, for example, other allies, specialists, donors, governments?	
6. Learning	**a. Key lessons** • What has your organisation learnt from its capacity building programme work? **b. M&E and learning methods** • What methods does it use to generate learning?	
7. Capacities	**a. Resourcing levels** • To what extent does your organisation invest in its capacity building work (money, people, space)? **b. Ways of working** • What ways of working has your organisation's introduced for this work? Greater field presence? More specialists in the field? **c. Knowledge development** • What investment has your organisation made in building up its knowledge of capacity building? Tools, methods, skills, language?	